To the lovers who love with bravery

And to Damaris, the soul whose profundity I only begin to understand

LOVE IS FOR THE BRAVE
e625 - 2023
Dallas, Texas
e625 ©2023 by Itiel Arroyo

All biblical citations are from New International Version (NIV) unless stated as another version.

Translated by Sophia Leys
Edited by Sarah Hauge

Designed by **JuanShimabukuroDesign @juanshima**

ISBN: 978-1-954149-49-6

Printed in the United States of America

CONTENT

PROLOGUE

I love reading, and I believe that it has allowed me to develop a certain intuition toward books. I used to judge them by their covers, but I soon discovered that appearance has nothing to do with essence.

"What do you value in a book?" I was recently asked in an interview. My response was, "Today, I value a book not by how much it fills my mind, but by how it accelerates my heart."

The book you have in your hands hits the mark by turning words into precise instruments that reach the heart, flooding it with life.

Writing about love is a difficult challenge because few words have been used, manipulated, and distorted as much as "love" has. I am grateful to God that Itiel Arroyo did not shy away from the challenge and decided to confront it. The result is in your hands, and I can assure you that it will not leave you indifferent.

I dove into the pages you are about to read. I did so with pleasure and tranquility, and upon resurfacing from that adventure, I was in love with love. The author describes love in such a way that it is impossible not to be captivated.

I want to highlight several things about *Love Is For the Brave*:

It is a straightforward book. It doesn't aim at a hundred targets; it only addresses one. It pursues nothing more—and nothing less— than revealing to the reader the essence and content of a reality as wonderful as love. And it succeeds!

It is a transcendent book while also being relevant. It is transcendent because it points to the sky, and relevant because it makes us tread on the earth. As someone once said, "To leave a mark, the first thing is to have your feet on the ground." This book is a guiding force that anchors us to land.

The language Itiel uses is biblical without being religious, approachable without being simplistic, direct without being rude, and contemporary without ceasing to be elegant.

Love Is for the Brave turns the Bible into a delightful collection of journeys. This book helps us travel fascinating routes to the heart of Scripture, where each story transforms into a real, close, and tremendously instructive experience for the reader. Yes, that is the other quality of the book you have in your hands: It extracts from the Bible life for the spirit and emotion for the soul.

For these reasons, and many more, you are about to embark on a pleasurable journey. Ingest and digest the wisdom of this book because I assure you that you will emerge from this voyage having grown.

José Luis Navajo

INTRODUCTION

Not always can we do great things, but we can do small things with great love.

Mother Teresa of Calcutta

When Luis first arrived in Kenya, he wondered how he and his fellow mission companions, all Spanish university students, could help in that hot African place. They boarded the plane without knowing what their mission would be upon arriving in Nairobi. It didn't matter if it involved digging a well, planting trees, or building a structure; they all had the same experience for it: none. However, Luis was certain that God had sent him to that place for a reason.

Eventually, they learned that their destination was to serve for a week in a hospice for dying children run by the Missionaries of Charity, founded by Mother Teresa of Calcutta. When Luis entered, he encountered a scene that broke his heart. He was in a dimly-lit shack, filled with stretchers and IV drips, full sick children, many of them so weak that they barely had the strength to cry out in pain.

Luis was literally stunned as he observed the sight. What could he do to alleviate so much pain? The lack of an answer left him paralyzed. Motionless. He felt useless.

Suddenly, a sister of charity grabbed his face with her rough, work-worn hands and, looking into his eyes with authority, asked him, "Have you come to look or to help?" That question was enough to unfreeze him. The woman then asked him to hold a two-year-old child who wouldn't stop crying. She told him, "Hold him in your arms and give him all the love you are capable of giving." Luis didn't quite understand what she meant, but he wanted to be obedient to the nun's request, so he lifted the child from the stretcher and held him. The child was so thin that Luis could feel his bones as he embraced him. He could literally see the movement of the heartbeat on the child's bare chest.

Luis remembered the way his sister would soothe her baby, and thought it might work here. He began to sing to the little one, to stroke his hair, to smile at him, and to give him kisses, as if he were his own child.

It was all he could think of, but he did it with all his heart.

The child stopped whimpering and smiled. A beautiful smile on a bony face dirty with mucus. A few minutes later, he fell asleep.

Soon afterward, however, Luis noticed that the child's chest had stopped moving. In panic, he rushed to the sister of charity who, placing her hand on the little one, confirmed his passing.

She knew from the beginning that the child was dying. She looked at Luis again, with eyes filled with light that contrasted with the darkness of that room. "This child died in your arms, and you, with your love, have preceded the love that God will give him for all eternity," she said.

Still holding the child's lifeless body in his arms, Luis began to cry and give thanks to God. In that moment, he understood the reason why Jesus had sent him there: to be able to offer in advance the love that God desires to give to people for all eternity.

THIS BOOK

When I heard Luis's story, the Holy Spirit spoke to me urgently: "I want you to precede divine love, to offer in advance a glimpse of the love God wants to give to people for all eternity. You don't need to go to Africa to do this; I want you to do it with the people I will put in your arms." Over time, I have come to understand that love, and being a carrier of that love in the midst of a world in agony, is a top priority.

Through the pages of this book, I invite you to join in this supreme calling. I do not do this in my own name—I do it in the name of

Jesus, the one who descended from heaven to this dark and dying world because of sin, and who showed us the love of God in advance.

With this book, my goal is to challenge you to become a bearer of God's love in your world. I have made an effort to be very practical in describing what it truly means to love the people in your surroundings, primarily your partner, your family, and your community. As you read, you will discover that true love is connected to other virtues, such as courage, honor, commitment, protection, and forgiveness.

TRUE LOVE CONNECTS WITH OTHER VIRTUES SUCH AS COURAGE, HONOR, COMMITMENT, AND FORGIVENESS.

Secondly, I want to apologize. This book is not a comprehensive work on the depths of love. I believe I only scratch the surface of a topic that will take me a lifetime and a significant part of eternity to uncover. Instead, I focus on describing what it means to love in the midst of some of the challenges presented by the important relationships in our lives. I also admit that it is somewhat challenging for me to write about the art of love when so often I fail in my attempt to love as God expects. Like you, I am learning.

In this book, I want to share my deepest desire. I pray that as you read, the great love with which you are loved will be revealed to you. I pray that you will discover Jesus, the lover of your soul. Because only by feeling completely loved can you have the courage to love others.

01

HESED

THE WAY GOD LOVES

PIERRE TEILHARD DE CHARD

THE DAY WILL COME WHEN AFTER TAKING ADVANTAGE OF SPACE, WINDS, TIDES AND GRAVITY, WE WILL TAKE ADVANTAGE OF THE ENERGIES OF LOVE FOR GOD. AND THAT DAY, FOR THE SECOND TIME IN THE HISTORY OF THE WORLD, WE WILL HAVE DISCOVERED FIRE.

Because I desire mercy, not sacrifice, and acknowledgment of God rather than burnt offerings.

Hosea 6:6 (ESV)

It is challenging for me to imagine a generation more confused than ours about what love is. We are constantly influenced by confusing messages about what love means.

I have heard some teenagers say that love is falling in love, mothers describe it as what they felt when they first smelled their baby's skin as they held their newborn to their chest, and fathers see it as making sure their children have what they need. Some spouses speak of love as respect, while some talk about love being shown through how people spend their time. Young people seem to focus on kisses and caresses, and the elderly value companionship and protection.

So, with so many different interpretations, what is love really? What does it look like?

Politics defines love as a right, biology as an instinct, and neurology as chemistry. Some claim that love is blind, others say there is love at first sight, and I have even heard that love justifies everything.

Honestly, it is easy to feel confused with so many definitions of what it means to love, especially when these definitions sometimes contradict one another. And while th s word remains undefined in the hearts of this generation, our world experiences a terrible shortage of lovers.

In fact, this confusion becomes evident when we consider the image that comes to mind for our generation when we talk about being a lover. Some people tense up just hearing the sound of that word. Have you noticed how this precious word has been distorted to the point where it has become something terrible?

In our current culture, a lover is seen as someone who engages in a romantic relationship with another person who is married, maintaining a secret relationship focused on seeking pleasure. Indeed, the word "lover" has become synonymous with adultery, lies, and betrayal. It is a word that leaves behind a trail of destroyed marriages, children poisoned with hatred, and even the abortion of unintended babies.

As if this distortion of the term were not enough, our culture has worn out the word by using it in absurd ways, to the point it has been robbed of all its power. We say, "I'm a lover of classical music" or, worse yet, "I'm a lover of hamburgers." Is it possible to use the same word to describe what we feel for a piece of meat and what we feel for a person?

WORDS HAVE THE POWER TO SHAPE OUR THINKING.

Although it may seem like harmless speech, I am convinced that words have the power to shape our thinking. To put it differently, a change in language leads to a change in mindset. If you pay attention to the sound of your inner voice, you will realize that whenever you think, you do so through the language you have learned.

In fact, as you read these printed words, the meaning you believe they have is shaping an idea in your mind. Therefore, the meaning they have for you will condition your way of thinking. Ultimately, what we think becomes what we speak.

THE POWER OF WORDS

This is a spiritual principle revealed in the Bible: Words have the power to create realities. If you pay attention to the opening lines of the Bible, you will discover the first attribute of divinity: God speaks.

In the poem of creation, we observe that God created the cosmos by speaking; He created reality through His words. God said, "Let there be light" (Genesis 1:3 ESV), and light emerged from the essence of His words. God continued to speak, and what He said was created through the power of His words. Before anything else existed, there was the mind of God, and when He put words to His thoughts, this reality we call the universe came into being. Space, energy, and matter arose from the words of the Eternal.

Let me give you an example to better illustrate this idea. If you take a smartphone and begin to interact with its applications through the screen, you see colors, lines, and shapes that, when combined, project an image, such as a sailboat sailing on the sea at sunset. Your eyes perceive that combination of colored pixels, and your brain interprets the image. But if you think about it, that image you see—that combination of colors, lines, and shapes, that boat, that sun, and that water—is a projection: the product of a programming language. In the deepest layer of that image, beyond the illuminated pixels on the device's screen, there is a binary code, a language formed by ones and zeros that, when combined in the correct way, create the reality you see. In other words, what you see on the smartphone screen is actually created by a language.

I imagine that when scientists manage to split the atom to its most fundamental essence, they will hear the sound of God's voice, the vibration of His words. Because that is what everything in the universe is made.

When God set out to create life, He created it through His words. He spoke to the earth, and it produced vegetation; He spoke to the water, and it produced marine animals. God spoke to each eco-system, and from them emerged biological life that would depend on that atmosphere to live. The environment from which they originated would sustain them. I cannot help but be moved when I think that when God created humans, He did something different from what He did to create everything else. God spoke to Himself and said, "Let us make mankind in our image" (Genesis 1:26 ESV). In this way, the spirit of man was produced from the essence of the Trinity, and it is sustained and dependent on that atmosphere to live. God is the habitat of the human spirit; therefore, the human spirit cannot survive apart from God, just as a fish cannot survive outside of water or a plant cannot endure without being rooted in the ground. It is true that God formed the body of the first human being from the dust of the earth, which is why our bodies require the nutrients of this ecosystem to stay alive, but our spirit comes from God and cannot survive if disconnected from divinity.

When God breathed His breath through the nostrils of that piece of clay shaped like a human body, He placed a part of Himself in man, a spirit in His image and likeness. And I will venture to say that one of the reflections of God bestowed upon human beings was language, that attribute that distinguishes us from any other animal on the planet Earth. Language gives us the ability to reason and imagine, to communicate with other human beings, imprinting ideas in the minds of those who hear our words, creating abstract concepts in thought, such as beauty, forgiveness, or dignity. It is through words that we define what is good or bad, just or unjust, true or false. We shape the world around us through language. Ultimately, through the gift of speech that God has given us, we create the concepts that will drive our souls, give meaning to our reality, and govern our world.

God gave us language so that we could continue His creative work. He gave us words so that we may use them to build a world that reflects His goodness. However, we can also do the complete opposite.

Satan is so aware of this principle that he uses it to create toxic realities that destroy human beings. In the first conversation Satan had with humans, he used words to twist their thinking about who God is. By subtly manipulating the words that God had spoken, Satan distorted their original meaning and made humans believe that God was untrustworthy. Satan's words literally shaped a toxic thought in their minds that ended up separating them from God. That is what he did then, and it is what he continues to do now: distort the meaning of words so that they no longer signify what God intended them to mean.

This satanic strategy is highly noticeable in the media. For example, in news broadcasts in Spain, the word "abortion" is not used, but rather "voluntary pregnancy termination." Likewise, the term "euthanasia" is replaced by "death with dignity." One day, during a conversation on television about the romantic affairs of celebrities, a commentator mentioned infidelity, and the host corrected him by saying it was "unfaithfulness." I have also heard interviewees share their versions of events by saying, "This is my truth."

But if there is one word that Satan has most taken upon himself to distort in our generation, it is the word "love." That is why, in this book, I dare to challenge you to restore that word to its original meaning by embodying it in your own life. I challenge you to become a "lover," but one according to God's design. Because true lovers are those who love, and the meaning of love can only be determined by the One who created it: God Himself, the One described in the Bible as true love.

HESED

I have begun writing this book by speaking about the power of words because it was through one word in the Bible that my understanding of love was revolutionized. I do not exaggerate when I say that my mind felt an impact when I discovered this Hebrew word. I literally had to rethink everything I thought about love and seriously question whether I knew how to love. The power of this word changed my reality.

I thought I knew how to love until this word painted a picture in my mind of a kind of love that I did not know. When I read it, I could closed the door to my room and, putting my face to the ground, prayed to God: "Forgive me for practicing such mediocre love, I pray that you teach me to truly love." Years have passed since that prayer, and I am still wrestling with the implications of that word and discovering what it means. I am referring to the word Hesed.

Hesed appears hundreds of times in the Bible. It primarily refers to the relationship God has with His people, but it also alludes to the relationship God expects His people to have with one another.

The mystery of this word that has captivated me is that it is untranslatable. Yes, you read that correctly. There is not a single word in any other language that fully represents the meaning of Hesed.

Its meaning is so deep and rich in nuances that translators have had serious difficulties translating it into Spanish. There is not a single word in my native language that fully represents the complete meaning of Hesed. Ultimately, translators have chosen to translate it in different ways throughout the entire Bible:

Mercy
Tenderness
Faithfulness
Goodness
Grace
Covenant

Some translators render it as "covenantal love" or even as "unfailing love." It is fascinating! Or at least it seems that way to me. Because the truth is, that word encompasses the sum of all those other words. Hesed is a type of love full of mercy, tenderness, faithfulness, goodness, grace, and covenant. It is a love that does not run out, that fights and persists. A love so loyal that it never gives up. Hesed is a word so wide, high, and deep that you can get lost in it.

You could dedicate your entire life to discovering what it means. Probably that is why I have written this book—because I want to better understand its meaning.

I need to know.

Why? Because, ultimately, Hesed is the way God loves me. And I believe there is no more important revelation for my soul than that.

THE UNEXPECTED QUESTION

A friend asked me an unexpected question:

"Itiel, if God appeared before you and offered to answer just one question, what would you ask Him?"

I am convinced that there are plenty of immensely important questions for humanity, such as:

What was the origin of the un verse?

Is there life on other planets?

What is the cure for cancer?

I don't know what your question would be. At the risk of seeming egocentric, the response I gave to my friend came from the depths of my being. It was almost a reflex.

"I would ask Him: How is Your love fcr me?"

Since I was a child, I have heard that God loves me. I have sung that God loves me and read that God loves me. I know it is the truth because the Bible says so and because Jesus became a man to tell us on the cross.

I do not ignore this fundamental truth. But I admit that my soul longs to hear it ir every possible way. I want to understand all the nuances of God's love for me. I want to feel it, to be filled by it, to be marked by it. I have come to understand that I have been created to be loved by God, and the more this truth takes root in the most fundamental springs of my identity, the higher my life will be elevated.

KNOWING I AM LOVED BY GOD SETS ME FREE.

Knowing that I am loved by God sets me free.

It sets me free from the fear cf failure, of falling, or of making mistakes.

It sets me free from the chains of people's opinions, even from the chains of my own opinions.

It sets me free from anxiety aout tomorrow.

Love IS FOR **BRAVE**

Knowing that I am loved by God makes me brave, because one who knows they are loved can love with courage, can give, serve, forgive, and honor—heroic acts in a world governed by selfishness.

The revelation of divine love is like wings for a bird. How sad it is to live crawling when we have been created to fly!

For that reason, the word Hesed has become so important to me. I want to discover its hidden meanings because Hesed represents the way God loves me. But furthermore, it is the way God expects me to love the people around me.

And probably that is the correct order, because you cannot love others with Hesed if you have not been shaken by the Hesed of God for you.

Being a person full of Hesed is my calling, and it is yours too.

GOD WANTS *HESED*, NOT RELIGIOUS SACRIFICES

During the time when Jesus walked the earth, the meaning of the word Hesed had become so distorted in the minds of people that it had ceased to produce the effect for which God had intended it. Satan had managed to steal the power of that term, using those who were supposed to protect it to do so. He distorted Hesed through the religious leaders, those who called themselves the "guardians of the word of God," but failed to preserve it.

In several instances in the Gospels, we read how Jesus was harshly criticized by the religious elite after associating with people stigmatized by religion: lepers, tax collectors, foreigners, prostitutes, and others who were wounded by the disorder of their lives. Jesus approached them when religion dictated that these people should be isolated. Jesus, the incarnate Word of God, raised His voice to reclaim the meaning of a word that had been forgotten.

"Go and learn what this means: 'I desire mercy, not sacrifice.'" (Matthew 9:13)

Jesus spoke these words referring to the prophetic discourse of Hosea (Hosea 6:6), where Hesed is translated as "mercy." What Jesus was telling them is, "If you are unable to understand the meaning of Hesed, you are missing the core of the divine message. For more than ritual sacrifices, solemn feasts, or liturgical worship, God wants Hesed. God desires to see embodied in you a love filled with compassion, loyalty, and tenderness, a love that does not give up on difficult people, but persists in embracing them until what is broken in them is fused with the warmth of Hesed. God longs for you to practice Hesed with one another before engaging in any other religious matter. If you do not grasp this priority of God, you do not accurately represent God in this world. Go and learn what this word means. Do it out of devotion to God and for His purposes in this world."

Jesus spoke these words many times and in many ways to the religious leaders, so much so that they wanted to kill him. And I believe the He continues to say it today. He still cries out with tears.

THE PRIORITY IN JESUS' SCHOOL

On another occasion, a teacher of divine law asked Jesus what the greatest commandment was. He asked this question because each teacher prioritized certain commandments over others, and these nuances distinguished the different rabbinic schools of the time. Some schools prioritized a certain way of dressing, others focused on the manner of performing purification rituals, and still others emphasized specific Sabbath restrictions. There were as many schools as there were different interpretations of a commandment! And all of them were divided and believed they were better than the others. This greatly angered Jesus, because while the teachers of the Law prioritized secondary details of divine law, such as tithing even the smallest mint leaves from their garden, they forgot the main thing: practicing Hesed.

Jesus gave a response to the teacher that would establish the priority of his rabbinic school: "Love the Lord your God with all your heart, with all your soul, with all your mind, and with all your strength, and love your neighbor as yourself." Jesus declared that this commandment was more important than all the burnt offerings and sacrifices (Mark 12:33).

Jesus made it clear that the entire divine message can be summarized in this commandment that has two directions: "love God" and "love your neighbor." It involves two relationships, a vertical one with God and a horizontal one with people. However, they are not two separate commandments but one. And if anyone tries to fulfill one direction while ignoring the other, they fail completely.

JESUS SHIFTED THE FOCUS FROM RELIGION TO RELATIONSHIP.

It is more important than all the sacrifices and burnt offerings that were performed in the temple of Jerusalem. This statement may not seem very impactful to you, but it was startling to the Jews who heard it at that time. Understand this: The entire Jewish identity was linked to the temple of Jerusalem and the rituals performed in it. The city revolved around it; it was the central building and the reason why Jews from all over would make an annual pilgrimage to Jerusalem.

Those sacrifices and burnt offerings had become their national identity, what set them apart from other people, what made them special in their own eyes. Then Jesus stands at the entrance of that place, points to it, and says, "God doesn't really care about all the animal blood they pour on that altar if they forget about love. The temple may be what moves your hearts, but love is what moves the heart of God."

The religious authorities wanted to kill Jesus every time he opened his mouth because he shifted the focus from religion to relationship, from sacrifice to mercy, and from the temple to the people. It was too revolutionary then and remains so now.

RECOVERING THE MEANING OF TRUE LOVE

I admit that I tremble at the thought of one day standing face to face with Jesus, when He will look at me with eyes that penetrate the soul and lay everything bare. I tremble because on that day, I will have to give an account of how I have lived the life granted to me on this earth, and in that encounter with Jesus, there will be one question that surpasses all others, the primary question in the school of Jesus: "Itiel, did you love people?"

I believe that in that conversation with Jesus, love will be the standard by which the greatness of my life will be measured. How I treated the hearts of the people around me will either elicit applause from the angels or make them look away in embarrassment due to my mediocrity. And although I know that Jesus' love for me is sufficient to save me, I want to perceive in His gaze an expression of satisfaction.

That's why I am restless with the question I want to answer in this book: What does it truly mean to love the people around me? Because this world speaks of love, but it does not resemble Hesed. Someone claims to love their children while being unfaithful to their spouse; another says they love their parents while living in a way that causes them worried, sleepless nights; another insists they love their partner so much that's why they control them, checking all their messages and sometimes yelling at them. I have heard many say that giving sex is giving love, as well as the notion that all different ways of loving are to be respected. But perhaps what frightens me the most to hear is that anything goes in love.

But no! Not everything goes! That kind of love is a distortion; it is not the original. It is nothing but another fallacy of the Serpent. Why? Because if you detach love from truth, it ceases to be true love. Because if you detach love from faithfulness, it ceases to be true love. Because if you detach love from responsibility, it ceases to be true love.

You cannot castrate the word Hesed: you have to accept it with all its implications. Otherwise, you will not have true love. And that is what the following pages are about: discovering the connections of love with sacrifice, forgiveness, patience, honor, and other virtues that make up the mosaic of what true love is in the significant relationships of our lives. Through different stories from the Bible, we will seek the answer to the question with which this chapter began.

I pray that you discover what Hesed is and that this type of love possesses you. Saint Augustine, the bishop of Hippo in the 4th century, said: "Love, and do what you will: if you keep silent, let it be out of love; if you cry out, let it be out of love; if you correct, let it be out of love; if you forgive, let it be out of love. May the root of charity exist within you; from this root, nothing but good can come forth."

A SCANDALOUŚ GENEALOGY

JESUS CAN WRITE A NEW CHAPTER IN YOUR STORY

02

These are the ancestors of Jesus Christ, descendant of David and Abraham: Abraham was the father of Isaac, Isaac of Jacob, and Jacob of Judah and his brothers. Judah had Perez and Zerah by Tamar; (...) Boaz had Obed by Ruth, and Obed was the father of Jesse. Jesse was the father of King David, and David had Solomon, whose mother had been Uriah's wife. Solomon was the father of Rehoboam (...) Jacob was the father of Joseph, who became the husband of Mary, and Mary was the mother of Jesus, the Messiah.

Matthew 1:1–3, 5–7, 16

The Gospel begins with a genealogy. For many, it is a boring list of names with no significance. It's likely that you might have skipped over that long list while starting to read. Perhaps you quickly glanced over it on your way to the real action, the birth of Jesus. I've done it the same thing many times—until I realized that this genealogy connects God's story with the history of our human failures. In starting the Gospel this way, God conceals a message.

To decode the hidden message in this genealogy, you must first understand what the Gospel is about. In summary, it tells the arrival of true love in the world, with God becoming part of human history by incarnating in Jesus.

It excites me to think about this: that Jesus is the Word of God made flesh, the word Hesed entering into skin and bones, divine love walking on the earth, touching the lepers, kissing the children, and embracing the prostitutes.

Jesus is *Hesed* in action.

Therefore, if you want to know how love speaks, you only have to look at how Jesus spoke. If you want to know what love prioritizes, you only have to look at what Jesus prioritized. If you want to know what angers love, you only have to look at what angered Jesus. Ultimately, Jesus is the true form of love, and any other form is a distortion.

Even though the protagonist of the Gospel is God, The Gospel begins with a scandalously human genealogy. This is because God does not want to disconnect His story from ours.

Behind each name, there is a story.

Real stories, of real people.

We must embrace this genealogy just as it is: the honest and uncensored testimony that Jesus was born into a dysfunctional family.

Undoubtedly, when God connects the story of Jesus with the history of His ancestors, it is because He is trying to tell us something.

A SHAMEFUL RESUMÉ

In today's Western culture, we show others our worth through our academic titles, our beauty, or professional achievements; that's what that tells the world who we are. However, in Jewish culture, at the time when Jesus was born, people's worth came through their genealogy. In those times, the history of your lineage—meaning the record of the people with whom you were connected through preceding generations—defined how others saw you.

Genealogy was a way of telling the world, "This is me." The genealogy was something of real importance and gave social standing. For this reason, people used to any dark deeds committed by their ancestors to avoid losing others' respect. It's like what we do today with our weaknesses: We divert attention from what embarrasses us, we cover up our imperfections, or we apply a filter to photos where we don't look our best. We want to show the world the best version of ourselves.

But the Gospel does the opposite with Jesus: It introduces him to the world through a genealogy full of dark episodes. The description of God's love coming into the world is preceded by a collection of names that evoke stories to forget. This Gospel exposes Jesus' genealogy as a list of people who failed miserably in their interpersonal relationships, who failed in the art of love.

I will only mention a few of the shameful events from the ancestors of Jesus:

Jesus was the descendent of Abraham, who out of cowardice handed his wife Sarah over to a pagan ruler, pretending she was his sister, to protect his own life.

Jesus was the descendent of Jacob, who deceived his blind father to usurp the birthright blessing from his brother Esau.

Jesus was the descendent of Leah, who was neglected by a husband whose heart belonged to her sister Rachel, and felt pressured to marry her.

Jesus was the descendent of Judah, who participated with his brothers in selling their younger brother Joseph as a slave to the Egyptians, while deceiving their father into believing that Joseph had been killed by a wild beast.

Jesus was the descendent of Perez, who was born out of incest between Tamar and her father-in-law.

Jesus was the descendent of Rahab, a prostitute.

Jesus was the descendent of David, who became obsessed with Bathsheba, the wife of one of his friends, and forced himself upon her, resulting in her pregnancy. David also orchestrated the murder of Bathsheba's husband to cover up his adultery

Jesus was the descendent of Solomon, who, seduced by pleasure, had hundreds of pagan wives that led his heart astray to idolatry.

I could go on, but I'll stop there.

As you can see, I'm not exaggerating when I say that this genealogy points to a family history full of incidents, betrayals, and immoralities so scandalous that any king would have wanted to hide them to preserve their image. But not Jesus. He doesn't care about being presented as part of a family tree full of people who failed in their human relationships, who didn't pass the test of love.

That's how He presented Himself to the world.

But why?

Because with this genealogy, Jesus is conveying a message of hope to all of us who have failed in our human relationships, who have not lived up to the demands of true love. He says to us, "I am the

Son of God, but I am also the Son of a humanity that has failed in its relationships as parents, spouses, children, and siblings. I can identify with each of your traumas, feel what a violated woman feels, an unwanted child, or a deceived father. I am God, but I have entered into human flesh to feel them, experience them, and suffer them."

Jesus identified with the failures of His ancestors and added his name to the genealogy. Even though it seemed impossible to bring something good out of such a story, when Jesus was born it started a new chapter.

And that's what Jesus wants to do with you!

He wants to be born in you.

Because when Jesus is born into a life, no matter how disastrous its history of interpersonal relationships may be, He can start a new episode. Jesus continues to identify with your own history, with the list of mistakes you made as a child. He sees your entire record and puts His name at the end. In other words, He can break the curse of your past and bless your future. When Jesus is born into a relationship, even if it is in ruins, He can rebuild it. His perfect love can make all things new.

Now every time I start reading the Gospel, I read each one of those names. Because I have understood that, just like in a mosaic, each singular piece draws a bigger picture.

HIS STORY

I have read the Bible several times, and I must confess that I have gotten lost on many occasions. It's easy to lose the central storyline and get distracted by the details.

I think that's why many have chosen to use the Bible as a book of instructions, like a manual for religious life or a collection of divine laws.

I admit it's simpler that way:

You open it somewhere.

You dissect God in the form of doctrines.

You extract some ideas to improve your life.

You expand your to-do list.

And you close it without your soul trembling.

You open and close the book without it igniting your heart, without stirring your insides, without sending shivers down your spine.

Why? Because you have lost the main thread, you have lost what makes it fascinating: the story behind the stories.

As my friend says, "If reading the Bible doesn't leave you in awe or intimidate you, then you're not understanding what you read. If you read the Bible without understanding what you read, it will have the same effect as reading the instruction manual for an appliance. But if you understand that the Bible is a story, the heart-rending, exciting, violent, tender, controversial, and captivating tale of a God who loves humanity, then it will hook you."

Good stories always captivate, and this is the greatest story of all.

But let me be clear: Although it is a love story, it is not a sentimental tale. Instead, it exposes the beauty and rawness of true love. Just as it really is. Uncensored. Because in this account, "love" is written as "sacrifices," with letters soaked in blood. Because the protagonist of this book dared to love us to the bitter end.

I haven't known a more courageous love than this.

OUR STORIES

Though the divine romance is the main plot, the Bible also tells the story of our human relationships, a collection of micro-stories within the grand story that expose our efforts to find a partner, deal with family tensions, be loyal to our tribe, show justice to the weak, or forgive those who have hurt us. It also talks about how we manage the emotions of love, the desire for revenge, the sting of envy. And, ultimately, it addresses the challenge of loving in a world corrupted by sin, or—better said—the great challenge of loving with a heart corrupted by sin.

Honestly, this sacred book narrates some human successes, but it exposes many more failures. If you open the Bible expecting to find idyllic romance, perfect families, or unbreakable relationships, you will be greatly disappointed. The Bible is full of honest accounts that, in the best cases, show imperfect people doing their best to love others, but, in the worst cases, reveal the rawness of human selfishness destroying everything around them.

If you want to indulge in a world of fantasy, do not read the Bible, because it will confront you with the stark reality of human nature—a reality that is as relevant today as it was then.

IF YOU WANT TO INDULGE IN A WORLD OF FANTASY, DO NOT READ THE BIBLE.

In short, the Bible highlights these two realities. On one hand, it reveals our inadequacy to love and how we continually fail to meet the challenges of loving our neighbor. On the other hand, it uncovers Jesus as the perfect lover, capable of expressing love to its fullest potential, displaying the extensive range of what it means to love others.

THE LOVE OF GOD IN US AND THROUGH US

Now, you might wonder: If our corrupted hearts are so incapable of fully loving, what's the point of trying? You could become discouraged by the reality of your condition and give up on the challenges that relationships present. You might resign yourself to the mediocrity of loving only yourself. So what's the point? It's this: God promises that if you persist in the challenge of love, Jesus will be born in you.

God doesn't expect us to love others based on the power of our love; He expects us to love others fueled by the power of Jesus' love working through us. This is not just a poetic phrase; it is a promise. God promises to make the spirit of Jesus dwell in us to transform us into lovers like Him. It is through this Spirit that we are empowered to love even when from a human perspective it seems impossible.

I want to be emphatic about this: We cannot love like Jesus if we rely on our own strength; we can only love like Jesus if He is born in us. Even your best efforts, noblest intentions, or most disciplined virtues will be insufficient for a task as immense as loving as Jesus did. We must humble ourselves and admit that without Jesus being born in us, there is no redemption for our history of failures. Without Jesus being born in us, our insufficiencies will add another embarrassing chapter to our family genealogy.

But if Jesus dwells within you, His love can drive you to accomplish great feats, heroic acts like forgiving an enemy, being faithful to your spouse until death, honoring imperfect parents, or sacrificing for someone else's benefit. I'm referring to the kinds of exceptional actions that, in a world accustomed to selfishness, will make people sense something divine in the way you love.

WE CANNOT LOVE LIKE JESUS BY RELYING ON OUR OWN STRENGTH.

That is what this book you hold in your hands is all about:

Letting the wild love of God possess you.

Allowing God's love to be expressed through you.

Loving dangerously and being a lover.

Like who?

Like Jesus. God's love is expressed fully in flesh and bone. There is no purer love than that, none more provocative, none riskier, none more attractive.

LOVING LIKE JESUS HURTS

It wouldn't be fair to you if, I didn't give you a serious warning here: Loving like Jesus hurts. Even though it is the spirit of Jesus within us that empowers us to love as God expects us to, this kind of love hurts. It hurts a lot, and God does not numb us. A few years ago, I traveled to Jerusalem for the first time. I was excited, thinking that I would visit the places that had witnessed the events I had read about so many times in the Gospels. I had idealized these places in my mind, and my expectations were high. However, while some of those places transported my soul into the presence of God, others rather transported me to a shopping center on a sale day. I had the unpleasant sensation that some of those places had been turned into a kind of religious attraction in a giant theme park.

One of the places where I had that feeling was the Garden of Gethsemane.

There were so many people present; they literally pressed me from all sides and spoke in all languages. They pushed and trampled on me, trying to take a selfie with an olive tree in the background. It was also so hot that I could smell the sweat on the stranger beside me. All of this was taking place while I heard tour guides shouting their explanations: "Here, Jesus lived one of his darkest nights," as a vendor added in the background, "Cheap prayer shawl for sale."

Horrible.

But when I returned to my room, trying to somehow redeem this experience, I opened my Bible to the passage that recounts what Jesus experienced in that place. From that room, I felt my soul transported to the reality of what happened on that night of pain.

That night in which it hurt Jesus to love us.

He withdrew about a stone's throw beyond them, knelt down, and prayed, "Father, if you are willing, take this cup from me; yet not my will, but yours be done." An angel from heaven appeared to him and strengthened him. And being in anguish, he prayed more earnestly, and his sweat was like drops of blood falling to the ground." Luke 22:41-44

I do not exaggerate when I say that night in Gethsemane was the moment that would determine the future of our relationship with God.

Thousands of years before, in a garden, a man named Adam decided to cross a boundary that God had established in Adam's relationship with Him. The result was a rupture that affected all of us, the descendants of Adam. The first name in our genealogy hides a very sad story, the story of how a bad decision can destroy the most important relationship. But that night, in another garden, a man named Jesus was going to decide if that relationship was worth all the pain it took to save it.

We say that Jesus won the battle for our salvation on the cross, and it is true. However, his sacrifice on the cross was the external result of an internal battle that he had already won hours before in Gethsemane. At some point in our lives, I believe that we can all identify a similar battle in our minds.

Imagine that a relationship is broken, and it is evident that the responsibility is not yours, but rather of the other person. They have betrayed you, been irresponsible, or offended you in some way. However, it is an important relationship, and you are aware of its value. Gethsemane represents that conflict that makes you question yourself: Is it worth enduring the pain that comes with saving this relationship?

When I speak of the pain that comes with saving a relationship, I'm talking about something difficult to explain in words—but our soul understands it very well. I'm talking about the pain of forgiving the father who, in your childhood, chose the bottle over taking care of you. I speak of the agony of swallowing all your reasons to distance yourself from that spouse whose words have been like daggers and continue to work on your relationship. I'm sure your soul knows what I mean.

Gethsemane hurts.

Gethsemane was an olive grove where Jesus used to have communion with his Father. But on that night, Gethsemane was not a place of communion; it was a place of decision.

The name Gethsemane is derived from the union of two Aramaic words, which translate to "place of pressing olives." In that garden, olives were pressed to obtain olive oil, which was much-needed for life in Jerusalem. But on that night, what was being pressed was the heart of Jesus.

A Jewish historian explained to me that in the Hebrew culture of that time, three pressings were done on the harvested olives, resulting in three different oils that were used for various purposes. The first pressing was done with the weight of the olives themselves pressing against each other. This first oil, considered the purest, was collected for use in the sacred rituals of the temple. The second pressing was done using the strength of a human body. This second oil, which was of high quality and good taste, was consumed by people, used in food and cooking. The third pressing was done using stone weights that exerted great pressure, crushing the olive and its pit completely. This third oil was bitter, so it was used as fuel for the lamps that illuminated the city.

It is interesting to note that the Gospel narrates that Jesus prayed to the Father three times in Gethsemane, in three different stages, each time under increasing pressure. The text states that Jesus was under such intense inner pressure that he sweated blood. The reader may be tempted to interpret this as nothing more than a poetic expression by the author, but it is not. Jesus literally sweated blood. Doctors call it "hematohidrosis": a physical condition when the inner pressure is so high, the anxiety and terror are so unbearable, the heart pumps blood with such aggression that the tiny venous capillaries in the skin burst, releasing blood that oozes through the pores of the skin.

Can you imagine the pressure Jesus was under?

The Father was revealing to Jesus the kind of pain he would have to endure to save our relationship. He showed him the whip that would tear his back, the crown that would be driven into his brow, and the nails that would crush his limbs. But above all, he let him smell the "Cup of Wrath," a prophetic symbol of God's judgment against sin, which Jesus would have to drink on that cross if he wanted to reconcile us.

This scene reminds me of a comment my wife made after returning from the dentist. She said, "If I had known how much it would hurt, I wouldn't have gone." I think that's why the Father considered it fair to let Jesus know what it would hurt to reconcile us with God, so that Jesus could decide whether or not to go.

What I'm trying to convey is that in Gethsemane, love is not about sentimentality, it's about making a decision: Does that relationship deserve all the tearing, humiliation, and agony it takes to save it? Jesus answered, "Yes."

Because pressure always brings out what you have inside.

When Jesus was pressed, he distilled a love so courageous that he endured the cross to redeem us.

Liquid love flowed through Jesus' skin in the form of large drops of blood, and those drops of love watered our withered relationship. A relationship that grows, and grows, and grows until it becomes a lush garden, a lost paradise.

LIQUID LOVE FLOWED THROUGH JESUS' SKIN IN THE FORM OF LARGE DROPS OF BLOOD.

So much love did Jesus distill in the press of Gethsemane that it is enough to feed our hungry souls and to illuminate the world.

And believe me, when the time of pressure comes, what you have inside will also come out of you.

YOUR GETHSEMANI

If you set out to love as Jesus did, aided by the spirit of Christ within you, you will inevitably have to endure your own Gethsemane.

You may protest and say, "But what if I don't feel like loving in that way?"

But dear reader, up to this point, who has spoken of feelings?

The truth is that love cannot simply be a feeling because you cannot give a command to a feeling. And God commands us to love as He loves.

For example, when I was a child, my mother would command me to eat my vegetables—but she couldn't command me to like them. Why? Because eating vegetables is an action, but liking them is a sensation.

Love cannot simply be a feeling because God cannot command us to feel something. Love is an action. And if it is an action, we have the power to decide whether to do it or not.

Love IS FOR **BRAVE**

Even if you don't always enjoy loving, even if you don't always feel like doing it, it is such a powerful action that loving can transform you and everything around you. Just by writing these words, I can feel my heart beating strongly within my chest, as if my soul were shouting, "Itiel, you were created for this." And indeed, there is no task that gives you more meaning than to love truly, even if it involves some kind of sacrifice. This is what you were created for.

03

SKIN TO SKIN

NO ONE IS AN ISLAND COM-
PLETELY UNTO THEM-
SELVES; EACH MAN IS A
PIECE OF A CONTINENT, A
PART OF THE EARTH. THE
DEATH OF ANY MAN DIMIN-
ISHES ME, BECAUSE I AM
LINKED TO HUMANITY; AND
THEREFORE NEVER ASK
FOR WHOM THE BELL
TOLLS, IT TOLLS FOR YOU.

JOHN DONNE

CONNECTION IS A MATTER OF SURVIVAL

The Lord God said, "It is not good for the man to be alone. I will make a helper suitable for him." Now the Lord God had formed out of the ground all the wild animals and all the birds in the sky. He brought them to the man to see what he would name them; and whatever the man called each living creature, that was its name. So the man gave names to all the livestock, the birds in the sky and all the wild animals. But for Adam no suitable helper was found. So the Lord God caused the man to fall into a deep sleep; and while he was sleeping, he took one of the man's ribs and then closed up the place with flesh. Then the Lord God made a woman from the rib he had taken out of the man, and he brought her to the man.

Genesis 2:18-22

The first chapters of the Bible describe the moment when God unleashed His creative power. God spoke, and from nothing, everything was made. Space, time, and matter emerged from the Word of God. Every particle of the universe is made of that essence, formed by the sound of God's voice.

When "Let there be light" occurred, scientists believe there was a release of a tremendous amount of energy in the form of a primordial soup of energetic interactions, where the first fundamental particles of the universe began to emerge. Through an incredibly long process, guided by the physical laws determined by the divine mind, the first hydrogen atoms, the most basic and lightest element, started to form from the initial chaos.

These first atoms attracted and pressed against each other, hundreds, thousands, millions, and billions of them, until, at a certain moment, they ignited the first spark of the most powerful nuclear furnaces in the cosmos: the stars.

When a star is formed, nuclear fusion reactions begin within it, a physical process in which gravity's pressure fuses atoms, transforming them into new atoms and converting lighter elements into heavier ones. This process releases a tremendous amount of energy in the form of light and heat. The primary fuel is hydrogen, which, through nuclear fusion, becomes helium, adding more interior pressure to the star's furnace. As the temperature at the center of a star reaches several million degrees, the transformation from helium to carbon occurs, followed by the transformation from carbon to oxygen, and so on, as the star illuminates the darkness of space. If the interior pressure continues to increase, other heavier elements such as magnesium, sulfur, silicon, nickel, cobalt, or iron can be formed. The majority of elements that make up galaxies are created within stars, through a process of nuclear fusion that spans millions of years.

And then, when all available fuel within the star is exhausted, the star, with its extreme size and temperature, collapses upon itself and explodes in the form of a cosmic blast known as a supernova. This explosion generates so much energy that it fuses some of the star's atoms, transforming them into the heaviest elements we know, such as gold. If someone gives you a gold ring, remember that when you wear it on your finger, you carry the remains of a star that once died.

This supernova launches into space as a "hurricane of stellar dust," known as nebulas, composed of those fundamental materials—those building blocks in the form of atoms—from which everything is constructed. The heavy matter begins to cluster and condense again, forming a new star from the elements of the exploded star, and around this new star, asteroids, satellites, and planets are formed. Planets like Earth.

DUST AND SPIRIT

In the reading of the biblical text, we can observe how God's creations become more complex, from energy to matter, from minerals to organic life, from plants to animals. The complexity of His creation increases as it moves from an initial state of disorder and emptiness to become perfectly structured and filled with life.

The existence of the laws that dynamize the universe and provide the order that sustains life is one of the most powerful pieces of evidence pointing to the existence of an intelligent designer. The more I learn about the fine tuning of each cosmological variable necessary for life, the more amazed I am by the mind of God.

On my journey toward knowledge, science has brought me even closer to God.

The poem of creation concludes with a beautiful image of God creating the human being, as if He were an artist shaping His masterpiece. God put His hand in the dust of the earth as he designed the human being. I like to think that He got His hands dirty when creating us, like a potter gets messy while molding clay on the wheel.

THE ORDER THAT SUSTAINS LIFE IS ONE OF THE MOST POWERFUL PIECES OF EVIDENCE POINTING TO THE EXISTENCE OF AN INTELLIGENT DESIGNER.

Then the Lord God formed a man from the dust of the ground and breathed into his nostrils the breath of life, and the man became a living being.

Genesis 2:7

There is something poetic about our origin when we think about the union of scientific knowledge and theological knowledge. When the Bible says that God formed our bodies from the dust of the earth, He did so using the elements that were forged inside the furnace of stars and released when they exploded. In other words, God formed us from stardust. In our skin, we carry the atoms that once formed part of the heart of stars, which one day died to provide the building blocks with which God would sculpt us.

When you gaze at the sky on a starry night, be amazed by the thought that you are part of the history of the universe—and that the history of the universe is a part of you. You are made of stardust.

And yet, within us, we find a longing that cannot be satisfied by anything made of dust. We desire something beyond atoms, beyond stars, beyond galaxies, and even beyond the universe itself. We are more than stardust, no matter how exciting that may sound; we are more than mere matter. God Himself breathed His breath of life into that clump of clay and placed His spirit within us. Divinity deposited a part of itself in us that desperately yearns to connect with God.

For that is how God created us, to be connected with the universe and to be connected with the divine. Stardust and spirit. We are atoms that contain a part of God Himself. We are a precious clump of clay kissed by God. But we became disconnected when we chose to be satisfied with dust-made fruit rather than God. Since those days, our souls have been starving.

Until Jesus arrived.

RESPIRATION

We were created with the vital need to connect with God.

When God breathed His breath of life through our nostrils, He not only activated the breathing of our lungs but also ignited our spiritual breathing.

I need to breathe oxygen; I won't forget that.

However, when I forget to breathe in the Spirit, God has left me a reminder in the sound of my breath.

Israel had various ways of referring to God, each with a special meaning. Elohim, Adonai, Shaddai, El Olam, and others, each revealing something particular about God's nature and character.

The special name by which God revealed Himself to Moses is YHWH. This name holds such great mystery and was considered so sacred that religious leaders prohibited its being spoken, except in very specific rituals performed by the priests. Over time, the exact pronunciation of this word was forgotten. On top of that, ancient Hebrew scripture did not include vowels for the word. Therefore, those four Hebrew consonants, known as the "tetragrammaton,"—YHWH—remained without a defined sound.

Various classical and contemporary authors point to a fascinating relationship between this sacred name and the sound of breathing. These letters would be pronounced one by one as follows: Yod - Heh - Vav - Heh. Now, the Heh is a letter that represents the divine *ruah*, meaning breath, wind, or spirit. This consonant is repeated twice in the name, giving the impression that "breath" is the main idea of the divine name. For this reason, many rabbis believe that the sound of God's name is the one that is produced within the human being when breathing deeply.

Perhaps for that reason, for centuries, when a scribe had to copy the sacred name, they would pause and take a deep breath. While you read this book, you are breathing, but you are also doing something more important—you are pronouncing the name of God. Even if you keep your mouth closed, even if you are an atheist or even if you refuse to pronounce it, you will still be speaking God's name. Inevitably. Because we start life by pronouncing the name of God with our first breath and end life by pronouncing the name of God with our last exhale.

We cannot live without breathing, just as we cannot live without God. These needs are fundamental. Perhaps for that reason, the last verse of the one hundred and fifty songs dedicated to God in the Psalms concludes, Let everything that has breath praise the Lord. (Psalm 150:6).

The breath of all living beings worships His name, because the breath of all living beings *is* His name.

NOT GOOD

All human beings have a vital need for connection with God. In addition, although it may sound scandalous (or almost heretical), God has created us with another fundamental need that not even He Himself can satisfy: the need for connection with other human beings.

It's not that God is limited in His power or unable to do what He wants, but the design He has given us requires this human connection. And God is at peace with that.

It's interesting to note in the text of Genesis that whenever God moved to the next day of creation, the Bible says: "God saw all that he had made, and it was very good." (Genesis 1:31 NIV). And yet, when creating Adam, He said: "It is not good."

"It is not good for the man to be alone; I will make him a helper suitable for him." - Genesis 2:18

I find it surprising that God said something in His creation was not good, especially considering He said this before the fall.

It seems that the only thing that was not good in paradise was Adam's solitude.

Was there something defective in Adam?

There was no defect, but he was incomplete.

Looking up, he could worship God, and looking down, he could rule over creation, but looking to his side, he was alone.

Adam's loneliness was not good compared to the rest of the created things that were complete.

God decided to create Adam with a fundamental need, a need that not even God could supply.

God created Adam with the need for companionship. With the need to connect with other human beings.

I believe you know what I'm talking about.

We long for true connection; we are desperate for intimacy.

God created us with the need for community, the need to relate to other humans. Even though it is possible to feel complete without a romantic partner, if we lack that human connection, we are terrifyingly incomplete.

Adam's loneliness was not good. God knew this from the beginning, but He wanted to make sure that Adam was aware of that need. Before giving him a companion, God entrusted Adam with the task of naming the animals. It was at that moment when Adam felt a void for the first time, one that not even the presence of God would fill. Perhaps he felt sadness in paradise, a place where it seemed impossible to be sad, given its impressive beauty and abundant possibilities and pleasures. Even there, it is likely that Adam arrived at the following conclus on: "What good is having everything if I have no one to share it with?" That feeling of emptiness was part of God's divine strategy to push Adam to establish a relationship with another. This feeling continues to push us to this day.

Loneliness was not good for Adam, and it is not good for you.

SKIN TO SKIN

We often talk about what a mother experiences on the day of her child's birth, but have you thought about what the baby experiences when being born?

Think about it.

For nine months, the baby has been in a protected environment, wrapped in a bag filled with amniotic fluid, at a stable temperature, without friction, surrounded by white noise. The baby is connected to the mother through the umbilical cord, constantly nourished in a dimly-lit environment.

I feel at peace just describing it.

And then suddenly, the baby's world is shattered. They come out of the mother's womb into an unfamiliar environment full of unknown, unfamiliar sensations.

The cold, the noise, the blinding lights, the feeling of pain when the doctor gives a little tap on the buttocks.

Can you imagine the emotional impact on the baby?

Midwives others who assist with childbirth are very aware of the stress the baby is experiencing they know the baby feels disoriented and unprotected. That's why, from the first childbirth until today, as soon as the baby is born, the midwife place the baby on the mother's chest to make them feel connected.

This is known as "skin to skin."

Before cleaning or even dressing the baby, the age-old wisdom of midwives attests that this contact is vital for the baby's soul. While the baby is on the mother, with their ear against her chest, they can hear the most familiar sound they know—the sound of their mother's heartbeat.

Today, after many scientific studies, we know that "skin to skin" has multiple benefits for the baby. The most immediate ones are that it helps regulate their respiratory and heart rate and temperature, alleviates the anxiety caused by birth, and promotes the initiation of breastfeeding. If all of this were not enough, it has also been proven that skin-to-skin contact improves the baby's cognitive and executive abilities and enhances their physical development, even years after it has been practiced.

I dare to affirm that from the moment we are born through the rest of our lives, we continue to desperately crave connection, to experience "skin to skin" with another human being, true intimacy.

> **FROM THE MOMENT WE ARE BORN WE DESPERATELY CRAVE CONNECTION, TO EXPERIENCE "SKIN TO SKIN"**

I have noticed that behind every surprise teenage pregnancy, there are desperate souls longing to connect with someone. Behind every foolish act of a young person in the presence of their friends, there is a desperate soul longing to connect with a social group. Even behind every conflict between children and their parents, there is a desperate soul longing to connect with authority. They are all trying to connect, but in the wrong way.

All of us long to connect with others, even though many times we don't know how, and we end up doing it the wrong way.

ISOLATION

It is not good to be alone. In fact, it would be more accurate to say that being alone is terrible. Loneliness can leave your soul crippled.

Isolation is a well-known form of punishment frequently used in prisons around the world. It can easily become a means of torture.

During the Cold War, there were rumors that China used isolation to manipulate prisoners. In the United States and Canada, the governments tested if the technique was a good weapon of war. Their defense departments funded a series of investigations that would be highly questioned today.

Researchers paid volunteers, mainly university students, to spend days or even weeks isolated in soundproof cubicles where they were deprived of any significant human contact. Their goal was to reduce sensory stimulation to a minimum, limiting what they could feel, see, hear, and touch. They then observed the individuals' behavior when subjected to this total isolation.

Journalist Michael Bond of BBC Future summarizes the disturbing results of that experiment. "Just a few hours passed, and the students became incredibly impatient. They needed stimulation. They started talking, singing, or reciting poetry to break the monotony. Many became anxious or highly sensitive. Their mental performance was also affected when performing arithmetic tests or word association tasks. The most alarming effects were the hallucinations."

The hallucinations began with points of light, lines, or shapes, eventually turning into strange scenes, like squirrels marching with sacks on their shoulders. The students had no control over their visions: one of the men only saw dogs; another, babies. Some also experienced auditory hallucinations, for example, a music box or a choir.

Others imagined that they were being touched, and one of the men felt like a bullet had hit his arm. When they came out of the experiment, they found it difficult to rid themselves of this altered sense of reality; they were convinced that the room was moving or that objects around them were constantly changing shape and size.

The researchers had to abruptly stop the experiment due to the volunteers' mental health. They had hoped to observe the subjects for several weeks, but the trial was cut short because the students appeared too distressed to continue. Very few lasted more than three days.

Isolation has a profound impact on the fundamental workings of the mind. Taking away human contact from the soul is as destructive as depriving the body of water.

Connection is a matter of survival.

DISCONNECTED

Obviously, the chances of experiencing total isolation today are very slim, but have you thought about all the ways in which our modern culture is disconnecting us from each other?

Not long ago, I was trying to have a conversation with a young man who was dealing with depression. He hardly felt like talking. It seemed that with every word he spoke, a little bit of life slipped away from him. I can't forget how he repeatedly said in despair, "I feel lonely, I feel very lonely." But if you had seen him a few months before, surrounded by people, you wouldn't have suspected that he was isolating himself inside.

It's possible to be surrounded by people but feel lonely on the inside. You can feel alone even when you appear to be accompanied.

I believe modern cities are fostering a type of social isolation that is becoming our padded cell. We might argue that we live in the "age of social media," but I think deep down we suspect that, although we are more connected virtually, we are more alone than ever. While the use of the internet is fundamentally communicative, it leads to a decrease in our face-to-face communication, a shrinking of our social circles, and an increase in depression and anxiety.

In our generation, the value of the tribe, community, or family—those precious social bonds designed by God to build our identity—is being lost and replaced by unhealthy individualism.

The Zulu language of South Africa has a term to define the importance of community in shaping a person: Ubuntu. An anthropologist proposed a game to the children of an African tribe. He placed a basket full of fruits near a tree and told them that whoever reached it first would get all the fruits. When he gave the signal to run, all the children held hands and ran together, and afterward, they sat together to enjoy the prize. When he asked them why they had run that way, knowing that only one could be the possessor of all the fruits, they responded, "Ubuntu." This word literally means "I am because we are," or in other words, "I am what I am because of what all of us are."

"It takes a village to raise a child," says an African proverb, but it seems that our generation in the West has believed that "the Internet is enough."

You were designed by God to connect with others, but to do it genuinely. The internet can be a supplement, but not a replacement for "skin-to-skin" relationships.

An emoji of a kiss on WhatsApp can never replace the warmth and moisture of lips on your cheek.

A "Like" on Instagram can never replace your father saying, "I love you."

A tutorial on YouTube can never replace your grandmother's advice.

A thousand followers on Facebook can never replace uncontrollable laughter with a couple of friends on the street.

A Twitter argument can never replace heated conversations with your family around the table.

Stop trying to "capture the moment" with your smartphone camera and *live* the moment. Be present, truly present, with other people. Disconnect from global news and connect with local experiences. Because when you're really having a good time, you won't remember to make a Story.

As I write these lines, locked in my room, I can hear my wife's voice and my baby's laughter in the background. I asked them to leave me alone to write, but not for too long. I need them, like water in the desert. I step out of this room from time to time to drink them in. I just remembered that it's my father's birthday; he's turning seventy-one. I'm going to call him on the phone to remind him that I need him, too.

Why don't you connect with someone now?

You were designed for that.

VIRTUES

God knew that Adam needed to deeply connect with another human being because the best virtues in our life can only be developed in community.

It is impossible to develop the virtue of generosity if there is no one to share what you have. It is impossible to develop the virtue of forgiveness if there is no one to offend you. And above all, it is impossible to develop the virtue of love in solitude. Love requires community; it requires someone to be expressed to.

This makes me think that when the Bible says, "God is love" (1 John 4:8), this is only possible because, from eternity, God is a community. The Father, the Son, and the Holy Spirit love each other eternally. They are connected. God has never been alone, and it was not good for Adam to be alone either. Because Adam's best virtues, which were still hidden within his soul like seeds planted in the soil, would only sprout in the atmosphere of companionship.

So, God subjected man to a deep sleep, took a rib from him, and with it, designed the most complex being of all His creation: woman.

I find it interesting that God did not allow Adam to participate in the process of creating Eve. I think He wanted to prevent Adam from thinking he was superior to Eve. If Adam had had the slightest involvement in the creation of woman or had witnessed how God made her, he would have faced the temptation to consider himself superior to her and her owner.

Using an allegorical interpretation of the Scriptures, Saint Augustine poetically reflected this idea by saying, "Woman was created from man's rib, not from his head to dominate her, nor from his feet to be trampled by him, but from his side, to be equal to him, under his arm to be protected, and close to his heart to be loved."

But we disconnected, because we chose to eat a fruit that was forbidden to us. That act, instead of uniting us more, put us in conflict.

Until Jesus came.

WHEN JESUS WAS TERRIFYINGLY ALONE

When I told that young man with depression that Jesus understood his pain, he asked me disdainfully, "What does Jesus know about how I feel?" To which I replied that Jesus knew the pain produced by loneliness because He was left alone on the cross. He experienced absolute loneliness. Jesus, better than anyone, could identify with his anguish.

I don't know if you had thought about this before, but the story of the Gospel is about how God saved us from "eternal loneliness."

We were created to feel complete while remaining connected to God and connected to other human beings.

But we chose to eat the fruit—we chose to cross the boundary.

We rebelled, and the consequence was disconnection.

Sin became the isolation cubicle for all of Adam's children, and we began to go mad.

If there's one thing I really want you to take away from these lines, it's that Jesus went to die on the cross to reconnect what Adam had disconnected.

On the cross, Jesus solved the problem of our isolation, but to do so, He had to face the greatest torture: to be left alone, terrifyingly alone.

> FROM THE MOMENT WE ARE BORN WE DESPERATELY CRAVE CONNECTION, TO EXPERIENCE "SKIN TO SKIN"

I want to be very clear about this. The greatest torture Jesus experienced on the cross was not the whip, not the crown of thorns, and not even the nails; the greatest torture Jesus experienced on the cross was to be disconnected from the Trinity. To be separated from God for the first and only time in all of eternity.

About three in the afternoon Jesus cried out in a loud voice, "Eli, Eli, lama sabachthani?" (which means "My God, my God, why have you forsaken me?"). Matthew 27:46

That was the agonizing cry of Jesus on the cross. At that moment He bore the sin of all humanity, and the holy God, who has no connection with sin, disconnected from Jesus. He left Him alone.

Can you even begin to imagine the terror that the one who had always been part of the Trinity experienced when He was disconnected? Can you get an idea of the pain that came from being left alone for the one who had always been united with God?

If there's a good definition of hell, it's probably this: the absolute absence of God.

Hell is eternal loneliness.

And Jesus experienced it on that cross for you.

What I told that young man, I tell you too: What kept Jesus nailed to that cross, enduring the pain of loneliness, was the hope of restoring a relationship with you. Don't be deceived by your feelings: You are not alone anymore.

EMBARRASSMENT AND APPEARANCE

04

YOU WILL ONLY BE ABLE TO TRULY CONNECT WHEN YOU GET NAKED

CONNECT

Adam and his wife were both naked, and they felt no shame.

Now the serpent was more crafty than any of the wild animals the Lord God had made. He said to the woman, "Did God really say, 'You must not eat from any tree in the garden'?" The woman said to the serpent, "We may eat fruit from the trees in the garden, but God did say, 'You must not eat fruit from the tree that is in the middle of the garden, and you must not touch it, or you will die.'" "You will certainly not die," the serpent said to the woman. "For God knows that when you eat from it your eyes will be opened, and you will be like God, knowing good and evil."

Then the eyes of both of them were opened, and they realized they were naked; so they sewed fig leaves together and made coverings for themselves. Then the man and his wife heard the sound of the Lord God as he was walking in the garden in the cool of the day, and they hid from the Lord God among the trees of the garden. But the Lord God called to the man, "Where are you?" He answered, "I heard you in the garden, and I was afraid because I was naked; so I hid." And he said, "Who told you that you were naked? Have you eaten from the tree that I commanded you not to eat from?"

Genesis 2:25, 3:1–5, 7–11

Eve joined the serpent in a dangerous conversation.

That's how all disasters in our lives begin: by having a conversation with the serpent.

What started with a seemingly innocent question ended in a rebellion.

The serpent didn't outright say what to do; the serpent insinuated. It planted the seed of doubt in Eve's mind. When Satan manages to sow one of his seeds in your mind, he gains a mechanism of control over you.

The serpent insinuated that God wasn't as good as He seemed.

The serpent insinuated that God was hiding something from them.

The serpent insinuated that God wanted to keep them prisoners.

And Eve believed it.

So, she took the fruit that God had forbidden them to eat and then offered it to Adam, who ate it too. And following that moment, something happened that would mark all their descendants until this day:

They experienced shame for their nakedness.

But hadn't they been naked from the beginning? Some rabbis maintain that Adam and Eve, before sinning, were clothed in light, covered with Divine Glory that literally radiated upon them. But when they disconnected from God, the source of their light, they were stripped of their brilliance. Completely naked.

This makes me think of the moon's supposed glow. Many lovers have been deceived while contemplating its brilliance, including me. I praised my girlfriend, saying, "You are more beautiful than the moonlight." But when you study a little astronomy, the romance fades away. The truth is that the moon doesn't emit light; it only reflects it. The moon is a giant gray rock orbiting the earth, and its glow is the result of being exposed to sunlight. The one truly radiating light is the sun. The moon is just a big, sad rock.

Adam and Eve shone while they were plugged into the source of divine light, but when they unplugged, they saw themselves naked and wanted to hide. They grabbed fig leaves, sewed them together, and made some makeshift clothing. Where there was once light, they put leaves that began to wither, which is how it always go when we attempt to fix things our own way.

The question is, who were they hiding from?

They were hiding from each other, covering themselves so that Adam couldn't see Eve's nakedness, and Eve couldn't see Adam's nakedness. They covered themselves so that the other couldn't see their shame.

They even tried to hide from God.

When God came to meet them, He asked Adam, "Where are you?" (Genesis 3:9), not because He didn't know where Adam was, but because Adam didn't know where he was.

SHAME

We were created with the fundamental need to feel connected to other human beings. But the biggest obstacle to achieving that longed-for connection is shame. Our shame is the greatest hindrance to intimacy with those around us.

We often confuse guilt with shame, believing they are the same, but they are not. Guilt is the pain we feel for something we have done, but shame is the pain we feel for something we believe we are. That's where their difference lies: Guilt is linked to behavior, shame is linked to identity.

SHAME MAKES US THINK:

"There's something wrong with me, something flawed and broken, and if others find out, they won't want to have a relationship with me." Shame makes us believe we are a mistake, not worthy of connection with others.

This book will end up in the hands of very different people, but if there is one thing all the readers of this book will have in common, I know without a doubt that it's shame. I wish it were otherwise, but I know that you feel shame. That shame is a mark on each of our souls, present in all the children of Eve.

God explained to Adam that the shame he felt in his soul was related to a voice he had heard. That's why God asked Adam, "Who told you that you were naked?" Genesis 3:11. God asked Adam about the voice with which his shame was connected, because shame always arises when we listen to and believe a wrong voice. That's why God asks:

"To which voice have you listened and believed?"

"To which voice have you given permission to penetrate your soul?"

"To which voice have you given authority to define you?"

This was the first moment when a human being was defined by a voice different from the voice of God.

The voice of the serpent.

The voice filled with poison.

The voice of lies.

WHEN YOU BELIEVE A LIE YOU GIVE THE LIAR POWER OVER YOU.

I'm not exaggerating when I warn about how dangerous it is to engage in a conversation with the serpent, even when it seems like innocuous dialogue. Satan's deception gives the ability to sabotage God's plan in our lives.

Why? Because when you believe a lie, you give the liar power over you.

Satan's words are like the legendary trojan horse, which on the outside appeared to be a gift, but inside hid a group of invaders ready to penetrate the walled city. Similarly, when Satan speaks to you, his words may seem true, but they conceal some lie. That lie is like a computer virus, in hiding until someone grants it access to their system and it contaminates everything.

If that lie from the serpent manages to penetrate to the foundational springs of your soul where your identity lies, and becomes a part of you, it will lead to shame. Shame arises when you accept a lie as part of your identity.

I remember a moment from my childhood that left me deeply ashamed. It was summer and I was about eleven years old. I used to play in the street with the neighborhood kids until the evening. A Nutella sandwich and a ball were all we needed for an epic afternoon. The norm in our group was lots of laughter and petty quarrels—typical for kids. That is, until one disagreement turned into a fight between another boy and me. A couple of insults and boastful threats were exchanged. It seemed like it would end there. However, as night fell, I was passing through an alley on my way home when the angry boy and five of his older cousins cornered me. What happened next caused me unforgettable shame. The biggest of them grabbed me by the collar and lifted me several inches off the ground, a position that made it hard for me to breathe. Fear paralyzed me. I didn't react; I just let it happen. At that moment, the angry boy pulled out a stick, like the ones used to prod horses, and began hitting me with it, encouraged by the rest of the kids, who laughed at me and insulted me, calling me a "trash bag." It's true that being hit like a piñata hurt, but I can assure you that the pain I felt in my body that night was not comparable to the pain I felt in my soul. I can't explain it, but that humiliating situation, where they treated me like a punching bag, made me feel violated. As if they were robbing me of my humanity. Perhaps you don't find it so serious, but as a child, my mind couldn't process what had happened. Somehow, a lie penetrated deep within me and brought forth shame. I was so ashamed that I didn't even tell my parents what had happened. For years after that, I hid from my aggressors, not because I was afraid they would hit me again, but because of shame. They knew something about me that kept me from holding my head high in their presence. Do you relate to what I'm talking about? If you've ever been shamed, I'm sure you do. The way shame emerges is strange, but when it does, it sticks to your soul until you start to believe it *is* your very soul. How cunning the serpent is.

LEAVES OF FIG TREE

Over time, I have seen how this pattern of behavior has repeated many times in my life, the times when I'll find myself doing everything possible to cover up my shame.

In the Church, we have learned to deal with feelings of guilt because, although it's difficult, we can repent for the mistakes we've made. But how do you deal with the feeling that arises when you are convinced that you are the mistake itself? How do you repent for something you believe you are? I have realized that what we do is the same as what Adam and Eve did: We

> **THE PRICE WE PAY, WHEN WE PUT UP APPEARANCES TO HIDE OUR SHAME, IS TRUE INTIMACY.**

choose to take control of our shame. We try to control what others can see of us.

They covered themselves with fig leaves to hide their shame from each other and God, and we cover ourselves with our image to do the exact same thing. When faced with shame we keep choosing to hide, only instead of sewing together a garment with fig leaves, we create an image to project to others.

We disguise ourselves as the best version of ourselves to conceal our deepest shames and project an image of perfection. We try to keep others from seeing our vulnerability.

Gradually, this turns our public life into pure theater.

The great tragedy is that every time we hide our true selves, we lose something we deeply long for: connection with others. From the moment Adam and Eve hid behind their fig leaves, they lost the connection they had with each other. Their intimacy was affected when they began to fear being naked in each other's presence. In the same way, every time we hide behind our appearances, every time we try to control the image we project to others, we pay a very high price: We lose true intimacy with the important people in our lives.

Ultimately, we end up feeling alone.

I want to emphasize this because I believe it is a great tragedy.

Putting up false appearances will condemn you to loneliness, even when you are surrounded by people. It is possible to work with people, eat with family, have thousands of followers online, and even have a partner and still feel terribly alone. The reason for this is that your soul doesn't crave companionship; it craves connection. But there is no way to connect with someone hiding behind your fig leaves.

CHARACTERS

One of our favorite ways to project an image is through social networks.

In reality, the internet has simply digitized our fig leaves, making it easier for us to control what others can see of us.

It has given us the opportunity to create a public persona to present to the world.

And it turns out that this persona is better than you and has a better life than yours. It is an improved projection of you. It's not who you are, it's who you would like to be. Or worse, it's who you think people expect you to be.

It's your persona, but I like to call it your disguise.

The other day, I caught myself doing something ridiculous. I'll confess it at the risk of you stopping reading the book once you discover how conceited I am. I was about to do my devotional. My Bible was open on the table and I had a cup of coffee in hand.

Then I thought, "What a spiritual image. I need people to see this." I prepared to take a selfie and upload it to my social network, accompanied by an inspiring quote, so that everyone could see how devoted I am. But after I took the picture, I realized it was too simple; I had to make it more beautiful. I grabbed a notebook, some markers, and some other books to decorate the table, making the scene appear more intellectual. But even the second photo didn't please me. I needed better lighting, to fix my hair, to hide the clothes that were lying on the floor. Before I knew it, I had taken ten photos. That's when I heard the Holy Spirit asking me, "Where are you?" (Genesis 3:9). After wasting fifteen minutes trying to keep my public persona up to date, I decided to delete the photos altogether.

The internet was not created to be a network of computers, but a network of people. It's interesting to note that the origin of the word "persona" comes from the Greek "prosopon," which means "mask." Honestly, I believe that one of the reasons why the internet brings together a global

community of millions of people is because it has allowed us to relate through the persona we have created. Social networks have become the great Venetian carnival of our time, a fantasy of characters presenting themselves to each other with their masks on.

It's no coincidence that we have a "wall" on Facebook and "filters" on Instagram, because don't secrets hide behind walls? And don't we use filters to hide imperfections?

If there's one thing that our era's social networks have shown, it's this paradox: we want to be known, but we're terrified of the idea of someone really knowing us.

We want to be seen, but not completely.

So we build superficial relationships, not from the core of our true selves. From the persona, not from the person.

And there's no way to achieve true intimacy with someone from the persona. Because it's a lie.

ADDICTED TO APPROVAL

Too often our public life, both online and offline, is just a performance.

Not long ago, my wife confronted me came to me, confronting me in the sweet and bitter way only she knows how to do. She said, "I don't want you to post any praises about me on your social network that you haven't said to my face, looking into my eyes."

This made me question my motivation for posting a picture of my wife enjoying the romantic dinner I had prepared for her.

"Did I do it to honor her, or to show everyone what a good husband I am and seek validation through their comments?"

I believe we suffer from the "Voice Syndrome."

I have no idea when you'll read this book, but as of the when I'm writing it, there's a highly successful television show called "The Voice," where contestants audition in front of a panel of judges to showcase their singing abilities. The twist is that the judges sit in chairs facing away from the contestant, so they can't see who is performing; they can only hear their voice. During the one-minute audition, the contestant must show the full potential of their voice, hoping that at least one judge will press the button on their chair and turn around. That's the signal that they've made it into the competition.

In a way, I think our generation suffers from this syndrome too. We want to be worthy of someone pressing the button; we want someone to validate us.

We crave approval.

Perhaps because approval is a relief from the pain caused by our shame.

Behind every perfect persona hides a person with shame.

I read the biography of a well-known TV host, someone who'd interviewed the most famous, wealthy, powerful, and distinguished people of her generation. She wrote that most of them, once the cameras were off, would ask her, "Did I do well?"

We are so fragile, even though we try to pretend otherwise.

We desperately seek human approval as a balm for our hidden shame.

Every time someone presses that button, double-taps your selfie on Instagram, likes your tweet on Twitter, or comments on your Facebook post, they are literally giving a stamp of approval to your soul.

It's super addictive.

So you strive to do even better, to look prettier, to appear happier, all in the hope that someone will press the button.

The other day, I logged onto a social media app and saw a picture of a friend hugging a beggar in one of the poorest areas of the city. As a caption, he wrote, "God won't give you the city you're not willing to embrace."

An epic photo with an epic caption. But honestly, what's wrong with our generation? In Jesus' time, when a Pharisee gave alms to a beggar, they would ring a bell to make everyone around them notice their act of generosity. We do something good and have to post it on social media for the whole world to see. Jesus called the former "hypocrites," which comes from the Greek word "hypokrites," meaning "actor." I think He'd say the same about the what we're doing today.

Believe me, if you live for people's approval, one day you'll die from their rejection.

Meanwhile, the one who truly pressed the button in your favor, not in a comfortable chair but on the cross, the one who made a sound for you, not with a bell, but with the nails that held Him to the wood with each hammer blow, is ignored.

Not a million "likes" could compare to that.

IMPRESSIVE

The Bible says we long to connect, but we confuse connection with impressing others.

We were designed to love and be loved, but shame makes us believe we are not worthy of that love unless we prove that we are impressive.

IT'S FUTILE TO TRY TO SATISFY YOUR NEED FOR LOVE WITH ADMIRATION.

Be honest: Isn't it true that many times you wear your virtues like a mask to impress others? Your profession, your social connections, your bank account, your branded clothes, your university degree, your theological knowledge. I certainly do. And it's exhausting.

As I get older and more mature, I can look back at my past and realize that many of the things I did to impress others were motivated by my need to prove that I was worthy of being loved.

After struggling with shame throughout my childhood, I discovered that I could gain some affection from people by getting impressive grades. I took school so seriously that I spent much of my adolescence locked in my room studying, all to get the highest grades on the next exam.

Please understand me: There's nothing wrong with being a diligent student. But now I realize that what I was seeking with those impressive grades was love.

Believe me, it's futile to try to satisfy your need for love with admiration. I've tried it, and it doesn't work.

Haven't you seen in the news how even people admired by millions end up committing suicide?

You can be impressive and still feel terribly lonely.

The time we spend trying to impress others is a real waste. At the end of our days, those we impressed will go on to be impressed by others. The only ones who will remember us are those with whom we truly connected.

You cannot love or receive love through the persona; you can only do it through the real person.

NAKED

In our hyperconnected virtual world, we feel more disconnected than ever. We long for a deep connection with others, but it seems like we can't achieve it.

I heard a sociologist say that we are suffering from an epidemic of loneliness. It makes sense. There's no way to deeply connect with someone while hiding behind our fig leaves.

To connect with another person, you have to be known, and to be known, you have to get naked.

To connect, you have to set your fig leaves on fire, stop hiding behind your appearances, kill the persona, take off the disguise, give up on trying to be impressive, and let yourself be vulnerable.

It's easy to take off your clothes and show your skin. What's difficult is baring your soul and letting someone see yourself as you truly are.

Fragile.

Imperfect.

Wounded.

Insecure.

Contradictory.

You, your true self.

I know! It's terrifying. But there's no other way to connect.

There isn't!

You must give up trying to control the image others have of you. You have to make yourself vulnerable.

"Vulnerable" is such a precious and yet chilling word.

The image it brings to my mind is that of a Medieval knight who comes home after war with his armor on. To enter the bedroom with his wife, he must strip himself of all his protection. If you think about it, he's more exposed in that room than he was on the battlefield.

Are you willing to be hurt occasionally in order to have connection?

Because the same armor that protects you from blows on the battlefield will also prevent you from experiencing the caresses of those who love you.

If you don't risk becoming vulnerable with someone, you won't achieve connection. Of course, it's not about baring your soul with just anyone, but it's important to connect with someone. Don't go through life just being accompanied; strive to deeply connect. The reward of intimacy is worth it.

To achieve that invaluable connection, you have to confront that question that makes even the bravest tremble:

"Will they still love me when they see me completely naked?"

I have answered that question at least in one relationship: the relationship I have with my wife. And don't deceive yourself! It's not in every marriage that both partners have seen each other completely naked. Not all have seen beyond the skin and past the layer of appearances. But my wife and I have. We have taken off our masks and revealed our secrets. What gives me security is that even after seeing me completely naked, she still loves me. In fact, I know that the deepest bonds forged between us have come through my shame, not through my talents. With her, I feel absolutely vulnerable, but at the same time, absolutely secure. It gives me great peace to know that she is more in love with me than impressed by me.

Trust me: anyone can kiss your skin, but you should stay with someone who kisses your soul.

THE CHURCH: A PLACE TO KISS SHAME

Recently, my wife gave birth to our first daughter.

While pregnancy is beautiful, it is also a great sacrifice. The body swells, the skin stretches, the bones wear out, and a significant number of hormonal changes occur in a woman's body. After giving birth, my wife felt uncomfortable with the idea of undressing in front of me and showing me her worn-out skin. I believe those who have experienced postpartum can understand what my wife felt at that moment. I understood what I needed to do to reconnect with her: I had to kiss those parts of her body that made her feel ashamed. And so I did.

In that moment, I wondered: isn't this what Jesus had in mind when He created His Church?

It was made to be a community where people could truly connect. A safe zone to take off the masks and show our naked souls. A place where shame is kissed by grace. A family where we can love and be loved.

Aren't we followers of the One who stripped Himself of His divine Glory and took on human flesh to be in contact "skin to skin" with us?

Aren't we followers of the One who, when tempted by Satan to throw Himself off the temple so that everyone could see how He would be rescued by angels, refused to be impressive?

WE ARE FOLLOWERS OF THE ONE WHO, BEING THE MOST INTELLIGENT OF ALL, SPOKE WITH SIMPLICITY.

Aren't we followers of the One who, though He was the most intelligent of all, spoke with simplicity so that people could understand Him?

Aren't we followers of the One who, having an army of angels at His disposal, showed vulnerability on the cross?

If we are His followers, let us learn to do for others what He did for us.

05

EXCLUSIVE UNITY

GOD WANTS TO SAVE YOUR WEDDING

So the Lord God caused the man to fall into a deep sleep; and while he was sleeping, he took one of the man's ribs and then closed up the place with flesh. Then the Lord God made a woman from the rib he had taken out of the man, and he brought her to the man. The man said, "This is now oone of my bones and flesh of my flesh; she shall be called 'woman,' for she was taken out of man." That is why a man leaves his father and mother and is united to his wife, and they become one flesh.

Genesis 2:21-24

It must have been an exciting moment when Adam woke up from his sleep and saw Eve for the first time. I can imagine the scene: Eve radiant, slowly approaching Adam, hand in hand with God. I believe the intensity of emotions that flooded their hearts at that moment can only be compared to what the bride and groom experience at their wedding: the groom waits for the bride to walk down the aisle and finally sees her approaching, given away by her father, who will release her hand to join it with his. Forever.

Indeed, this was the first wedding in humanity.

I love weddings! When I atterd a wedding, I always feel like I am witnessing something sacred. Something that evokes the dream of Eden, before sin messed everything up.

It's easy to get distracted, as if it were just another social gathering, where people dress in their finest attire, eat plenty of food, and try their best to look good in photos.

Ties, heels, flowers, tablecloths, and dances.

They are all just an excuse to show off and see others do the same.

But wait—let's not forget about the bride and groom.

It's easy to lose focus and miss the mystery, what is about to happen between the two of them, in that place, at that moment, with those witnesses: Two souls are about to become one.

That is why a man leaves his father and mother and is united to his wife, and they become one flesh. Genesis 2:24 NIV.

It is more than two people signing their names on a legal document; it is a deep and transcendent connection. A connection so sacred that God is more involved in it than in any other religious rite.

GOD ENJOYS WEDDINGS MORE THAN RELIGIOUS RITES.

Have you noticed that the Bible begins with a marriage and ends with a marriage? Genesis 2 tells the story of Adam and Eve's wedding, while Revelation 19 describes the wedding of Jesus and the Church. A wedding is the beginning and the end of the book.

In a wedding, we are witnessing a ceremony that recalls the ideal of Eden and projects the hope of the redemption of the universe. It is one of the few reflections of paradise we still have in this fallen world where we wait for the restoration of all things.

In fact, I dare say that God enjoys weddings more than religious rites. Because marriage was God's idea, not man's, whereas religion was man's idea, not God's. That is why, even though God is not present in some religious rituals, He is present at every wedding. Even if not invited.

It has happened to me so many times while I am standing there, watching the bride and groom look at each other as they make promises of fidelity. I can hear God whispering in my ear: "Take off your shoes, for the ground you are standing on is holy."

God is there. I know it, and even unbelievers suspect it.

UNDER THE CHUPPAH

In the times of Jesus, when a Jewish man loved a Jewish woman, he would marry her under a Chuppah. The Chuppah was a kind of canopy supported by four poles at its corners, which was held over the bride and groom during the wedding ceremony. That cloth over their heads was not just any cloth; it was a Tallit, a prayer shawl that Jews placed over their heads to remind them of God's presence over them as they recited the Scriptures.

This tradition connects with the time when God liberated the people of Israel from slavery in the land of Egypt and led them through the desert to the promised land. God covered them during the exodus with His divine presence in the form of a cloud by day and a pillar of fire by night. This presence over them protected them from the harsh weather, provided them with food, and scared away their enemies. Under that presence, God made a covenant with the at Mount Sinai and said, "This is my law and my promises, do not turn to other gods because you are mine and I am yours."

Those words are the language of weddings, the words of a groom reciting his vows to the bride. In Hebrew culture this is known as the Ketubah, the public oath the groom makes to the bride under the shadow of the Tallit, where he commits to her protection, sustenance, and care.

A testament that the bride will keep as a guarantee.

Upon reading this narrative of God and the Israelites, every Jew would have understood the idea that God had married Israel on that mountain. It was not the beginning of a religion, but of a marriage.

God's plan was always to marry us.

The wedding Chuppah evoked that special moment of God with His people. The same God whose covering extended over His people was now extending cover over the couple getting married. While the shadow of the Tallit was over their heads, they were aware of God's presence over them. God was with them in that transition, just as He was with Israel during the exodus. And, like at Mount Sinai, under that presence, a covenant was being written as the bride and groom exchanged their vows.

He would be hers, and she would be his.

In sickness and in health.

For richer and for poorer.

Forever.

God is the living Chuppah.

EXCLUSIVE UNION

During the wedding ceremony during the time of Jesus, only the couple remained under the canopy. Marriage is a zone of exclusivity for two, and there is no room for three. Marriage is a sacred union because it is an exclusive union.

Have you noticed that even those who claim not to believe in marriage get emotional at the wedding of a couple who does believe? Do you know why? Because they can perceive the beauty, value, and purity of what is happening:

A man and a woman meeting their beloved at the altar, saying "No" to all others to say "Yes" to one, forever. Rejecting all other possible options. Betting everything on one card. Declaring that "out of the seven billion people on the planet, I choose you and only you to give myself to in a unique way that I won't with anyone else."

We all can perceive the power of that act, which is why it moves us. We are witnessing the creation of something unparalleled that will belong exclusively to them. The sacredness of that bond derives from its exclusivity.

As I write these lines, there's a reality show on television based filming people for the first month of their arranged marriage, capturing moments of the couple on their honeymoon, learning to live together in their new home, and doing everyday things like shopping.

Caressing and kissing each other.

Arguing and shouting.

Apologizing and reconciling.

I have to be honest, I got hooked when I saw a couple arguing about how to place clothes in the closet. That is captivating television, and I'm sure it would have fascinated you too if you had seen it. It's easy to get hooked on this show. In a way, our soul knows that we are doing something forbidden by watching: We are violating the exclusivity of a marriage.

We are spying on the private moments of a couple.

Obviously, the network pays a high price to the couple to publicly broadcast their married life. But even though they may not realize it at the time, it is the couple who pays a higher price. They give up their confidentiality, the secret of their intimacy, the mystery of their union, in exchange for money. And when they have sold what was only theirs, it is no longer just theirs. It loses its value. They have allowed too many people under the Chuppah, and the likely consequence is that they will end up outside of it.

They may have money, but they no longer have exclusivity. They have irreparably profaned that sacred place.

Now, I am waiting for the program that broadcasts their divorce.

When I got married, I realized that what makes my marriage valuable are the details. The position we take while sleeping, the quirks we display while preparing breakfast, the way we divide household chores, how we manage space in the cabinets, how we fold socks, the affectionate nicknames, the way we say things to each other with a glance, the heartfelt discussions, the important days, the everyday routine, the meals with the in-laws... I could go on and on with seemingly insignificant things that have ended up becoming important. All of that and much more is ours and only ours.

Exclusively ours.

And there lies its value.

Therefore, we must be careful not to invite those in who shouldn't be under the canopy.

The secrets are ours and not your friend's as well.

The arguments are ours and not your mother's as well.

The longing looks are ours and not your coworker's as well.

The depths of your soul are mine, and the depths of my soul are yours. All this depth to explore is ours. It is part of our spiritual, emotional, intellectual, physical, and material union.

Genesis sums it up with a very meaningful word in Hebrew:

Yada.

Adam knew his wife Eve. Genesis 4:1 NIV

The word "Yada" has been translated into Spanish as "to know," but its amplified meaning is "to know completely and to be completely known."

"To know" in Hebrew means much more than accumulating information about the other person; it refers to experiencing the other person. Symbolically, it could be represented as the act of swimming in the depths of another person's soul. "Yada" evokes exclusive access to the secrets of the other's heart.

Recently, I participated in a Jewish-style wedding, and I was fascinated by how they concluded the ceremony. Wine was served to the bride and groom in a crystal cup, and both drank from it until not a drop was left. Then, the bride placed the cup at the groom's feet, and he stomped on it, breaking it into pieces in front of everyone as the hall filled with shouts of joy. This peculiar custom can be interpreted in different ways, but I believe one of the most beautiful explanations is that it highlights that no one else will drink from that cup that the couple has shared. Nobody else will be able to use it. It will be their exclusive cup forever.

PASSION IN THE NUPTIAL CHAMBER

In the time of Jesus, after exchanging their vows, the couple was not yet married. They needed to be accompanied by their families and friends to the place where they would seal their union, a very special tent called the nuptial chamber. The chamber was specially prepared to facilitate the sexual union of the couple, with a table full of fruits, sweets, and wine, carpets and cushions, and a bed adorned with all kinds of special touches.

Without a sexual union, there is no union of souls.

There is no marriage.

A kiss on the lips was the public signal of what the couple would do in the privacy of the nuptial chamber. Because, then and now, sexual relationships begin with a kiss. The bride and groom's wedding kiss was the first of the dozens they would share in the following minutes. Of the millions they would share in the coming years.

This sexual encounter was expected, desired, and demanded by the witnesses. Until that encounter took place, the wedding celebration did not begin. There was no emergence of a new family without a sexual union, so there was nothing to celebrate until that intimate encounter occurred.

That's why the family members placed the Chuppah over the nuptial bed and waited outside while the union was sealed through sexual intercourse.

Yes, you read it right: the family waited outside, singing songs to inspire the bride and groom. The father and the mother-in-law. Without any shame, but with their approval. Sex was not designed to be an uncomfortable secret, something done covertly in a motel room. It was designed as something intimate for marriage, yet worthy of celebration by the important people in the couple's life. Sex was never intended to produce guilt before God, but to bring joy to His heart.

Under the Tallit, they caressed each other passionately, pressed against each other in an embrace so intense that their skin almost melted into one another and they caressed each other's souls. They glided over each other's bodies. Looking into each other's eyes, they breathed each other's breath, discovered the taste of each other's lips, and the smell of each other's hair. Under the presence of God, they made love, because God is the God of love. And the God of sex. Because God created sex for love. In conclusion, sex in marriage is something worthy, blessed by the presence of God, and celebrated by the family.

In that time, when the newlyweds left the nuptial chamber, their parents entered to look for signs of the bride's virginal blood on the bed to validate the marriage. Understand this, even if it makes you uncomfortable. Although true virginity is more related to the soul than the body, the shedding of blood is often involved in the sexual act of a virgin couple. Because, for God, marriage is not a human contract signed with ink; it is a spiritual covenant sealed with blood. For in God's world, every covenant is confirmed with blood. That is spiritual.

I would dare to say that nothing is more exclusive in a couple than their sexual encounters. It belongs to them, and it should not be shared with anyone else. But a society where sex is projected on screens, sold on the internet, and practiced without commitment, it is easy to forget that sex is spiritual.

We have been made to believe that it is just physical.

We have been led to think that it is just an exchange of fluids.

We have been convinced that it is just instinct.

We have been presented with sex as mere mating, like in a National Geographic documentary. In fact, many of the sexual encounters in our culture are too similar to that.

How we talk shares how we think:

"Don't trust that snake."

"She's a vixen in bed."

"I fell prey to her charms."

"It was a wild night."

Reducing sex to something animal.

Without any transcendent purpose. Pure biology.

But God says that sex is spiritual. In fact, few things are as spiritual as sex. It is a mysterious union where souls merge while bodies unite.

The two become one person. Genesis 2:24

This mysterious union of two individuals who still preserve their individual identities but at the same time become one being points to something that transcends us. Therefore, God demands that these sexual encounters take place within the marital covenant. To protect the connection.

It is worth fighting to preserve that spiritual bond. And few things are more attacked by Satan than that special connection.

ECHAD

The Bible says that God expects His children to reflect in this world who He is, or rather, who He is Then God said, "Let us make human beings in our image, to be like us. They will reign over the fish in the sea, the birds in the sky, the livestock, all the wild animals on the earth, and the small animals that scurry along the ground." So God created human beings in His own image. In the image of God He created them; male and female He created them. Genesis 1:26-27

In the ancient Near East, in the context in which these words were written, temples were places of worship, and it was believed that the presence of a particular god resided within them. In these sacred places, an idol made of stone, metal, or wood was placed to represent the "visible image" of that god. In this way, people could know what that god looked like, what it represented. The Garden of Eden was a sacred place, a place filled with the presence of the true God, but in this temple, God d d not want an idol to represent Him; He wanted the human being to be His "image." If someone wanted to know what God was like, what He represented, they only had to look at man. In fact, we can see how the Ten Commandments expressly forbade making a representative image of God because, for God, only the human being is His image. That was the original plan, but Sin distorted it.

But, which of the two was the more accurate image of God? Man or woman? Who represented Him better?

The answer lies in the word "echad."

"Echad" is the Hebrew word used in Genesis 2:24 to say that Adam and Eve became "one." It is the same Hebrew word used in Deuteronomy 6:4 to say that God is 'one."

Can you grasp where I'm heading?

Adam was created in the image of God and represented Him in this world in many ways. Eve was also created in the image of God and represented Him in this world in many other ways. However, the union of Adam and Eve was the ultimate representation of the Trinity on Earth.

Adam and Eve were one, just as God is one. In their union, they reflected the nature of divinity, as inexplicable but beautiful as the mystery of the Trinity. Therefore, the purpose of marriage is not marriage itself but to point to someone beyond them: God. Their union is an image, a reflection of what God is.

We can notice God's desire to reflect Himself through marriage in the fact that the writers of the New Testament constantly challenge us to take the relationship that Jesus has with the Church as a marital model. It's as if God commissioned them, saying, "Be my message to the world; let your marriage tell the world what the Trinity is filled with."

How?

This concept is beyond our human comprehension, just as the mystery of the Trinity is beyond our understanding. However, in the intimate union of a man and a woman, there is a glimpse of something profound and divine. It echoes the unity and love that exist within the Godhead. When a husband and wife come together, in their own limited way they reflect the perfect union of the Father, the Son, and the Holy Spirit.

The oneness they experience is a symbol of the oneness of the Godhead. It is a reflection of the perfect love and unity that God desires for His creation. As they love and serve one another, they mirror the self-giving love that flows within the Trinity.

Marriage, then, becomes a sacred institution not merely for the happiness of two individuals but for the purpose of reflecting the divine mystery and love to the world. It is an invitation for others to catch a glimpse of the eternal relationship between the Father, Son, and Holy Spirit, the echad of God.

In a world that often misunderstands the true meaning of marriage and seeks to redefine it, believers are called to display a counter-cultural witness through their marriages. By living out God's design for marriage, they become living testimonies of the love and unity found within the Triune God.

When we see a husband and wife love, honor, and cherish each other, we should remember that it goes beyond them; it is a reflection of the divine love that binds the Father, the Son, and the Holy Spirit together in perfect harmony.

When a marriage breaks in the Church, the Gospel loses credibility before the world. It's about staying united when separation would be the easier option. When the world sees that despite difficulties, the husband and wife still believe in each other, that despite offenses, they forgive each other, and that despite other options, they choose each other again and again, then the world can understand that the Trinity is filled with this: perseverance, forgiveness, and commitment. In other words, God expects marriage to be the Gospel that others can read, not by telling a perfect story, but by telling the story of love that endures. Love that doesn't give up.

It's not a coincidence that Jesus prayed for His disciples a prayer that was as urgent then as it is now: "that they may all be one, just as you, Father, are in me, and I in you. that they also may be in us, so that the world may believe" (John 17:21). What Jesus was saying is that unity is a matter of credibility before the world. When divorce rates in the Church are exactly the same as in the larger society, our message loses credibility. Perhaps the acceptance in our churches of divorce as a valid option to solve problems has been one of Hell's greatest victories.

A few months ago, this tragedy happened again: Two of our friends got divorced. They were a committed couple in the service of the local church, a beautiful couple in the eyes of their friends. Obviously, they had their challenges, as every couple does, but they were seen as a couple that complemented each other very well. When they told us they had decided to divorce, I nearly choked on my coffee. I couldn't believe the argument they used to justify the end of their marriage.

They said, "The love is gone. We're just great roommates; there's no passion between us anymore." To which I responded, "Love didn't end, you stopped putting in the effort to keep it alive. Love is not like the energy in a battery that gets used up with time, love is like a plant, whose life depends on being watered. You simply stopped wanting to take care of the plant you both planted on the day of your wedding."

I don't want to be insensitive to those who decide to end their marriage because I understand that there are reasons for divorce. When violence, abuse, or infidelity poison a relationship, they kill love. I am concerned, though, that our generation assumes that divorce is a good option to solve cohabitation problems. Perhaps this cowardly way of loving each other is inspired by a consumer society that quickly discards what breaks and buys something new.

For my wife and myself, the first year of marriage was difficult. Uniting two people into one always involves friction. My own foolishness provoked more than one argument. For example, my ridiculous idea that I could still maintain bachelor habits while being married, like deciding what time I went to bed. I still remember when my wife was getting ready to go to sleep and invited me to join her. She was convinced that being married meant going to bed together, but I was used to staying up late, and refused several times to go to bed so early. This led to exasperated words from my wife: "If you wanted to live like a bachelor, you shouldn't have married me." Although my wife was right, my pride made me respond: "Well, maybe I shouldn't have married you, then." The concerning thing was not the disagreements, but that we made it a habit to threaten each other with divorce. Although we didn't really mean it, we used that threat to manipulate the situation. This went on until one day when the Holy Spirit confronted me harshly, saying, "There will be no future for your marriage until you remove that word from your vocabulary." After that confrontation, I understood that for those who truly love, divorce is not an option. We agreed never to use that word again in our discussions. Now when we fight, we have no choice but to fix it because running away is no longer an option.

God expects that one day we can look at our partner and exclaim: "She is bone of my bones and flesh of my flesh." In the Bible, bones refer to strength and flesh to weakness, so it could be translated like this: "In what I am weak, she is strong, and in what she is weak, I am strong."

God knows that if we fight for our unity, we can become inspire the world. Unity does not come from a fleeting relationship. Unity is the reward of a covenant.

JESUS, THE SAVIOR OF WEDDINGS

In Jesus' time, after the ceremony, the celebration finally began. The Jews were experts at celebration. A marriage meant a public feast for the whole community, a week of songs, dances, and laughter; the celebration by which the bride and groom would be remembered in their community. It was an event that reflected on the couple's entire extended families.

With this background in mind, we can understand that the Gospel of John presents a significant incident that occurred during a wedding in Cana of Galilee.

On the third day, there was a wedding in the village of Cana in Galilee, and the mother of Jesus was there. Jesus and his disciples were also invited to the wedding. The wine ran out, and Jesus' mother said to him, "They have no more wine.' - John 2:1-3

For the Jews, the fact that the wine had run out at such an important social celebration was not an oversight that would go unnoticed. In a honor-based culture, running out of wine represented shame for the family. Wine was the most important element of an Eastern banquet, and probably, it had run out when there were still a few days left of the celebration. If the wine ran out, the party would end, and the laughter of the bride and groom would turn into tears.

Hearing this, Jesus identified with the pain of this couple and performed a miracle. He turned six hundred liters of water into wine, enough to extend the party for as long as needed and save the family's honor. The wine was of such good quality that it earned the couple praise from the community. The Gospel describes this miracle of turning water into wine as "the first sign of Jesus."

Now, we all know that the purpose of signs is to point to something more important than the sign itself. If you get absorbed in looking at the sign, you might miss what it's pointing to.

So, what was this sign pointing to?

Why was Jesus' first sign to save a wedding celebration by turning water into wine?

Because Jesus was pointing to His own wedding. To that moment when the Church, you and I, His beloved bride, will be eternally united with Him.

Let us rejoice and exult and give Him the glory, for the marriage of the Lamb has come, and His Bride has made herself ready; it was granted her to clothe herself with fine linen, bright and pure. - Revelation 19:7-8

By saving those newlyweds from potential shame, Jesus was pointing to the time when there will be nothing to be ashamed of. That sign pointed to the hope of the universe when we will be united with Jesus forever and return to paradise to celebrate our wedding.

Where there will be no more pain, sickness, or suffering.

Where there will only be tears of joy.

Where death will have died.

A place where there will be wine for everyone eternally.

Every time a wedding is celebrated in this world, it is a sign pointing to the Great Wedding.

THE COST OF THE WEDDING

For Jesus, the cost of this Great Wedding has been very high. I believe this teaches us something about what a marriage costs.

Adam was put into a pleasant sleep to receive Eve, but Jesus was subjected to a terrible death to receive the Church. Adam was opened in his side; the price he paid to obtain his wife was a simple rib. Jesus was opened in his side, and the price he paid to obtain his wife was every drop of his blood.

We cannot focus only on the first sign of water turned into wine and forget the last sign of the cross. The first pointed to hope, but the last pointed to the cost.

If marriage represents the story of the Gospel, then it is a story of when someone loses their life so that another can gain it.

I am tired of sentimental views of marriage! Marriage is many things, but it's sentimental. Marriage is a beautiful sign, but also a painful one. Marriage is the embodiment of the Gospel with all its implications—and if I recall correctly, the Gospel is all about Jesus persisting in loving us despite our betrayals, being patient with us, forgiving our mistakes, being faithful despite our indifference. and keeping passion for each one of us until the end. There is no Gospel without the cross, nor marriage without sacrifice.

THERE IS NO GOSPEL WITHOUT THE CROSS, NOR MARRIAGE WITHOUT SACRIFICE.

It is not a coincidence that in our culture we use the expression "bring to the altar" as a synonym for marrying someone, because both a marriage and an altar are the place where sacrifices are made to God. Any sacrifice made for love in a marriage is an offering to God.

But Jesus, the Bridegroom, reminds us of something we must not forget: that although the cost was very high, when the Father brings the radiant Bride and joins the couple's hands, every sacrifice will be rewarded eternally.

06

SNAKES AND STONES

GOD DOES NOT BLESS THOSE WHO DO NOT COVER THE SHAME OF THEIR PARENTS.

Noah, a man of the soil, proceeded to plant a vineyard. When he drank some of its wine, he became drunk and lay uncovered inside his tent. Ham, the father of Canaan, saw his father naked and told his two brothers outside. But Shem and Japheth took a garment and laid it across their shoulders; then they walked in backward and covered their father's naked body. Their faces were turned the other way so that they would not see their father naked.

When Noah awoke from his wine and found out what his youngest son had done to him, he said, "Cursed be Canaan! The lowest of slaves will he be to his brothers."

Genesis 9:20–25

This is one of the strangest stories within the Bible.

The event described in these verses occurred just after one of the most severe divine judgments witnessed by humanity: the great flood. It was a cataclysm that brought an end to life on planet Earth as it was known until that moment.

The Bible says that leading up to the flood, the hearts of human beings had become so corrupt that all their thoughts were evil. The scenario described is dreadful. Violence, deceit, and lust were the human culture. It became so unbearable for God that "it grieved Him that He had made man, and His heart was filled with sorrow" (Genesis 6:6).

The judgment against wickedness was not a sudden divine outburst. In fact, God's patience had extended for centuries, waiting for people to repent of their evil deeds. But they did not, and the flood was a response commensurate with the dimensions of the evil that had flooded the earth.

Amid all of that darkness, God found a small glimmer of light: the heart of a man named Noah. God decided that the flood would sweep away all plant, animal, and human life from the face of the earth, except for what would be preserved in an "ark of salvation," a large boat built by Noah and his family, which would serve as a refuge for the seeds and animal species that would repopulate the new world along with them. God would start His story again with mankind, trusting that the descendants of Noah would not follow the same paths as the descendants of Adam.

But soon after Noah, his family, and the remaining plant and animal life disembarked to begin a new history, we come to this unexpected episode. Noah, the righteous man who had shown himself to be different from the rest of humanity, planted a vineyard, made wine, and got drunk.

The man chosen by God to begin a new humanity, drunk.

The story does not mention that Noah drank wine and was in a jolly state. Rather, he got completely intoxicated, so drunk that he lay uncovered inside his tent. There was the man of God, unconscious, naked and unable to stand, lying in a shameful state on the ground in his tent.

It was a humiliating scene. Noah, the chosen one to redeem human history, drunk.

Let's analyze the context, for it's easy to judge Noah. Have you thought about the reasons that might have driven him to seek solace in alcohol? Take a moment to ponder. Noah had to witness all those people he had known throughout his life be annihilated by God's judgment. Certainly, they were wicked people, but some of them were his childhood friends, neighbors, or even relatives. In fact, we know that Noah tried to persuade them to repent, which implies that there was some affection toward them in his heart.

Imagine the moment when the door of the ark closed supernaturally and it started to rain.

Imagine how many people went to the ark and desperately pounded on it, saying, "Noah, open up!" But Noah couldn't open a door closed by the hand of God.

Imagine how Noah heard from the other side the cries of mothers carrying their babies, begging to enter.

Imagine the heart-wrenching screams of those who knew they were going to drown.

Just imagine it.

This is not a story to tell children while they draw the ark filled with animals; this is the testimony of the extermination of a generation. And, as harsh as it may sound, it was a just judgment.

Perhaps that shocking scene was imprinted in Noah's memory. And though we don't know for sure, perhaps Noah drank to forget. After all, Noah was a man with weaknesses, like all of us. Whatever the reasons, we know what happened: Noah got drunk.

And then Ham, one of Noah's sons, went to his father's tent and saw him naked, lying on the ground in that embarrassing situation. Instead of helping him, Ham judged him. He looked at his father with moral superiority and judged him for his drunkenness. And not only did Ham judge him, he also left his father lying there, abandoned Noah to his fate.

And then he had the brilliant idea to gossip about it to his brothers.

In response, his brothers did something very different. They took a cloak, put it over their shoulders, and walked backward to avoid seeing their father's nakedness. They approached him with compassion and covered him in his shame. Showing respect toward their father, they avoided seeing him naked and covered him with kindness despite his indignity.

THE RELATIONSHIP WITH OUR PARENTS WILL TEST THE QUALITY OF OUR LOVE.

When Noah woke up and learned what his sons had done, he blessed those who covered him, but he cursed the son who judged him and left him abandoned.

There is a relationship that none of us choose, one that is imposed on us from the moment we are born. I'm referring to our relationship with our parents. I care to say that it's this relationship, more than any other, that will test the quality of our love.

This unavoidable test for our hearts, which will reveal our true inner nature, is based on whether we will honor imperfect parents, even when their shameful nakedness is exposed before us.

Through the sad story of what happened between Ham and Noah, God wants to warn us that a generation that does not know how to cover the "nakedness" of their parents is a cursed generation that will not prosper. When I refer to the nakedness of parents, I mean their mistakes, their moral failures, and their displays of weakness. In other words, their flaws. God asks us to honor them despite their imperfections, to treat them with dignity even when we discover their weaknesses. To cover them with the cloak of compassion, respect, and tenderness when their shortcomings leave them lying on the ground in shame.

FOR SOME MISERABLE REASON, WE FIND PLEASURE IN FEELING MORALLY SUPERIOR.

How difficult it is to honor someone we know so well!

Though Ham might have been disappointed by Noah's mistake, it was no excuse for dishonoring his father. I believe that Noah's mistake was a test for his son's heart, because it is in situations like these, when our parent's shame is exposed before us, that the quality of our love is revealed. It is easy to honor people when we only know their virtues, but the test of love comes when God commands us to honor those we know too well. Those we have seen contradict themselves, lose their tempers, fail in their promises, and fall short of their values.

Those whom we have been observing since the day we were born.

Our parents.

How simple it is to look down on a father lying on the ground with moral superiority! For some miserable reason, we find pleasure in feeling morally superior to those who have authority over our lives. Deep down, even if we don't want to admit it, it makes us feel justified. The voice of our judgment drowns out the voice of our conscience, which reminds us of our own mistakes. Sadly, I have seen so many children take a pedestal of moral superiority and judge their parents' shame, attacking them with acts of disdain. Years later, I have seen those children become the very image of what they once judged so harshly. Experience has shown me that you always become that which you judge without compassion.

It is true that Noah got drunk, but in the list of heroes of faith in the book of Hebrews, his name stands out. On the other hand, the name of Ham, the son who dishonored him, was linked to a curse that affected all his descendants. For this reason, the law in the He-brew community established that the cursed son should be stoned outside the city to prevent the curse from spreading to the next generation. That's how serious dishonoring parents was considered. I know this may be particularly surprising for a generation like ours, where disrespect for elders is common.

The apostle Paul wrote a letter to Timothy, his beloved disciple, in which he prophetically described the type of people who would be on Earth before the end of times.

He wrote in his list:

"They will be lovers of themselves and of money.

They will be boastful and proud.

They will scoff at God and consider nothing sacred.

They will not love or forgive and will slander others.

They will have no self-control.

They will be cruel and hate what is good.

They will betray their friends, be reckless, and full of arrogance.

They will love pleasure rather than loving God."

In this list that describes a terrible kind of people—very similar to those who were judged by God in the flood—what always strikes my soul is finding "disobedient to their parents" mentioned. (2 Timothy 3:2).

DISHONORING PARENTS IS A SIGN OF THE DEPRAVITY OF A GENERATION.

Evidently, dishonoring parents is a sign of the depravity of a generation. If we are capable of that, we are capable of everything else.

CURSE

I can't get out of my head the last words of the Old Testament, the way the book of Malachi ends before the arrival of Jesus. The prophecy declared by the prophet Malachi says, "He will turn the hearts of the fathers to their children, and the hearts of the children to their fathers; or else I will come and strike the land with total destruction." Malachi 4:6 NTV

The prophet connects the state of the relationship between parents and children with the state of the land, meaning that, according to the prophet, the curse on the land is related to the disconnection of the hearts of parents from the hearts of their children. It's as if he is saying, "What happens between parents and children, the way their hearts respond to the challenges that arise in that relationship, will affect the destiny of the world."

That chapter of the book, more than any other, presents a test of love that will determine the curse or blessing of our world. It is not only talking about restoring the relationship between parents and children but also about healing the Earth.

It might sound like I'm exaggerating, but I think it's clear here that the Bible emphasizes honoring parents as a primary matter to God, and emphasizes that dishonor is a transgression with serious consequences for the one who commits it—and, ultimately, for society.

The divine ordinance to honor parents is included among the ten commandments. The first four commandments establish guidelines for our relationship with God, and the last six establish guidelines for our relationship with our neighbors. The commandment to honor parents is the fifth, right in the center, and is the only one that comes with a promise. And what a promise it is! It's the promise of long life and prosperity. I have always believed that God had to incorporate such a reward for fulfilling this commandment because He knew it was the most difficult. It's as if every child needed extra motivation for that one. I find it striking that the first human relationship mentioned in the ten commandments is the relationship with our parents. It's as if God is trying to tell us that how we respond in this primary relationship will determine how we respond in others.

Some time ago, I read some statistics in a popular magazine that made me understand why the relationship with our parents is so decisive. Apparently, eighty percent of the people who end up in jail for attacking others had a dysfunctional relationship with their parents. In God's law, "honor your parents" comes before other commandments like "do not steal," "do not bear false witness," "do not covet your neighbor's wife," or "do not kill." This is probably because someone who starts by attacking their parents, someone who is capable of deceiving, insulting, or assaulting their parents, will be capable of committing all sorts of evil against others.

Let's be clear: no one becomes a criminal overnight, but it is a slow process that begins at home, when we determine how we will respond to our parents.

And I say this aware that the situation that many have experienced in their families may have been very complicated. There are parents who are true tyrants.

The question is: what kind of person do you want to become?

Because your heart's response to the injustices you experience in your family will determine the kind of person you will later be.

The Bible says, "Whoever curses their father or mother, their lamp will be snuffed out in pitch darkness' (Proverbs 20:20). This means that dishonoring your parents makes you a certain kind of person, a person whose inner light is extinguished.

When I read these words, I always imagine a lit candle that someone places under a glass dome. In the first few seconds, or even minutes, the flame continues to burn brightly as if nothing has happened, but as the oxygen inside the dome gets depleted, the flame loses strength until it completely goes out. Similarly, dishonor encloses your inner light within an airtight dome. At first, it may seem like you are still shining, but if you don't break the dishonor in your life, sooner or later, you will be consumed and end up in utter darkness.

STONES AND SERPENTS

Your heart's response to the injustices you receive from your parents will determine the kind of person you will become. Remember that diamonds, before becoming precious stones, were simple pieces of coal subjected to immense pressure. Significantly, pressure was the mechanism through which they underwent a transformation. Similarly, the type of heart that learns to truly love emerges in situations of conflict, under the pressure of injustice. It all depends on our response.

This reminds me of a question that Jesus once asked parents:

"If your children ask for a piece of bread, do you give them a stone instead? Or if they ask for a fish, do you give them a snake?" Matthew 7:9-10 NTV

Sadly, I have known some parents who have given stones and serpents to their children. Parents who, consciously or unconsciously, have thrown stones of judgment at their children and poisoned them with the lies of the serpent. Some children decide to keep those stones and serpents and end up passing them on to the next generation, perpetuating the curse in the family.

However, other children become regenerators. They take those stones and build a private altar where they worship God in the midst of injustice, and they take those serpents and use the venom to create medicine for their family. These children turn the curse into a blessing, break cycles that may have been repeated for generations, and create new dynamics in family relationships.

When my wife and I were about to get married, we were aware that we still carried some stones and serpents in our backpacks, and we were determined not to perpetuate certain dynamics that we had experienced in our families. Our parents were good and undoubtedly did their best, but they were imperfect. They, too, carried certain stones and serpents inherited from their own parents. But we came to the conclusion that a good way to honor our parents was to become regenerators. So, we prayed to God for His Spirit to help us in such a difficult task. It's easy to perpetuate the curse, but turning the curse into a blessing is a daunting task. We took judgment and turned it into worship, praying, "Thank you, God, for our parents, because you chose them to bring us into life, and Your plan is perfect."

We also took the lies and turned them into medicine, praying, "Help us, God, to turn all the suffering caused by the poison of the lies we believed into medicine to heal others, so that every experience we lived through may serve to make us soul doctors."

Several years have passed since that prayer, and we continue to strive to transform the curse into a blessing. Now that we have a baby, we don't want to fill his crib with stones and serpents.

JUDGES AND EXECUTORS OF PARENTS

I imagine that Noah was an excellent father in many ways, but one day he crossed the line, got drunk, and ended up lying naked on the ground. I don't know if you have ever seen your father or mother losing control after having a few too many drinks, but surely you have witnessed other embarrassing situations.

You saw your mother humiliate your father while they were talking.

You caught your father in a lie.

You observed your parents behaving immaturely.

You were a victim of their outbursts of anger, and they unjustly punished you.

You never heard them ask for forgiveness.

In short, you know very well that your parents are imperfect. You know who they are better than anyone, because you have been observing them since the day you were born. You could easily make a list of all their mistakes.

But when the nakedness of your parents is exposed before you, how you react determines what kind of heart you have.

Will you cover their nakedness with a mantle of honor, or will you judge them and leave them lying on the ground?

I am concerned that the spirit of Ham is increasingly in our generation. There are too many children who look at their parents' shame with moral superiority and judgment.

Not only that, but children also become judges who punish their parents. There are many ways in which children can punish their parents without resorting to physical violence. Some punish them with silence and decide not to talk to them. Others punish them by withholding physical affection; they do not hug or kiss their parents and avoid even minimal physical contact.

Others punish their parents by excluding them from their lives, not allowing them to know their grandchildren or limiting contact. There are also those who mock their parents when they see them struggling to use new technology, those who shame them in public, those who raise their voices, and those who look at their parents with disdain.

I knew a man who had cut off all communication with his father for ten years. In that time, he had moved to another city, gotten married, and had a daughter, but his father knew nothing about all of this. When asked, the son said that was his punishment for having been an absent father.

All of them justify their dishonor by thinking, "They deserve it." They are convinced that their parents' inability to be the parents they demanded them to be gives them full right to punish them.

If you are one of these children, are you ready to be judged with the same severity with which you judge your parents? Because as Jesus said, "For in the same way you judge others, you will be judged, and with the measure you use, it will be measured to you" (Matthew 7:2).

You will end up becoming the image of what you judge without compassion.

UNCONDITIONAL HONOR

Discovering the importance God places on honoring parents and the effects of dishonor in my life was decisive in changing the way I looked at my dad.

A new lens that allows us to see others through God's eyes.

Honor is precisely that: a new way of looking at our parents. Honor is a new lens that allows us to see them through God's eyes and not through the perspective of their mistakes. Honor is about giving high value to our parents, not based on what they may seem to be, but on what God says they are. Honor means elevating them, giving them special treatment, and celebrating their life simply because they are our parents, and that is enough.

But it took me eighteen years to understand this.

I didn't realize how important all of this was to God until He responded to one of my prayers with a forcefulness I didn't expect. I was asking Him to promote me to higher levels of responsibility in His Kingdom, to serve Him passionately. But He said, "The conduct of your heart toward your father disqualifies you from serving in my Kingdom's affairs."

My dad was a typical Spanish father. He would leave home very early in the morning and return very late at night. He was responsible, very responsible, working all day to provide for the family's needs. But my dad had difficulty expressing affection to his children. He didn't know how to give a hug or say, "I love you." He was emotionally castrated. But, of course, how could he express affection when the only contact he received from my grandfather was a kick in the backside?! At the time, I didn't understand my dad's background; I couldn't grasp that he carried stones and snakes inherited from his own father. I just compared him to my expectations and disapproved of him in my heart, again and again.

My dad was a very rough man and often argued with my mom. Many nights, unbeknownst to them, I would hear them arguing in their room. They would talk about divorce on Saturday, and on Sunday at church, they acted as if nothing had happened. I thought they were hypocrites. Some nights, I would hear my mom crying inconsolably, and that built up offense in me toward my father. For many years, resentment was my dominant feeling.

That, among other reasons, is why I passed judgment and declared him guilty. Even that wasn't enough; I needed to punish him for not meeting my expectations.

So, for years, I executed my punishment with my silence, disdain, and constant criticism. When it comes to punishing parents, a child knows how to inflict pain.

That was me, someone who believed himself to be a victim, but behaved like an executioner. I demanded to be understood and embraced, yet I never tried to understand or embrace. I was becoming the living image of what I judged so harshly.

When God told me that I was disqualified from His Kingdom's affairs because of the conduct of my heart toward my father, I had the audacity to respond, "My father doesn't deserve my affection because he hasn't earned it." Then, God exhorted me, saying:

"Honor is unconditional. I don't expect you to honor your father because he has earned it; I expect you to honor him because he is your father, and I chose him to bring you into life. That is enough to deserve your respect. If your love falls short in this, it falls short in everything else in my Kingdom."

Unconditional honor?

I could assume that someone with an exemplary life is worthy of my honor, but to honor someone solely because of their position of authority over me? My mind couldn't accept it at that moment.

Over the years, though, I have come to understand that one can honor someone and not deny the evidence that this person may not have lived up what a parent should be. Honoring parents doesn't mean condoning what is wrong, allowing oneself to be humiliated, obeying orders contrary to divine principles, or tolerating abuse. Instead, it's about the posture of your heart toward them, giving them value and respect, refusing revenge, and repaying evil with good. I know it's difficult to accept the principle of unconditional honor toward parents, but they are significant people in your life, even if they haven't lived up to the moral standards of their position.

Honestly, I didn't like that conversation with God, which was repeated several times that year. I fought against His Spirit for months, refusing to break my dishonor. But eventually, I understood that the dishonor in my life was hindering God's purposes for me. I remember well the night I things changed.

I came back from a retreat. As usual, my dad had gone to bed before my mom and was already lying down. I opened the door to his room and surprised him by jumping on him. I suppose the scene looked a bit odd, but that's how it happened. I jumped onto his bed, while he tried not to lose his composure. I apologized for all the years I had judged him without compassion and hugged him tightly while crying on his chest. At that moment, my dad started crying too, "No, son," he said, "forgive me for not knowing how to show you affection when you needed your father's words and embrace, but you know how I am." Then, I did something that broke the dishonor in my life forever. I got down on my knees at the foot of the bed, in front of my father, and said, "Dad, bless me." My father was very surprised by my request, and although I suppose he felt a bit uncomfortable with the situation, he must have thought that he had no choice but to comply. So, he placed both his hands on my head and began to pray for me. He only used the few words he knew how to, but they were enough for my soul.

As that was happening, I noticed how my way of seeing my father began to change. You understand what I mean; my dad didn't change, what changed was my way of seeing him. He remained imperfect the next day, with the same difficulties expressing affection, but now I could see him with tenderness, through God's eyes.

That night, I heard God's voice saying, "Because you honored your father and broke your dishonor, I will release the calling in your life to serve your generation."

I know that it's thanks to the decision I made that night that you are reading this book today. I'm convinced of it.

So come on! Take that stone and crush the serpent's head.

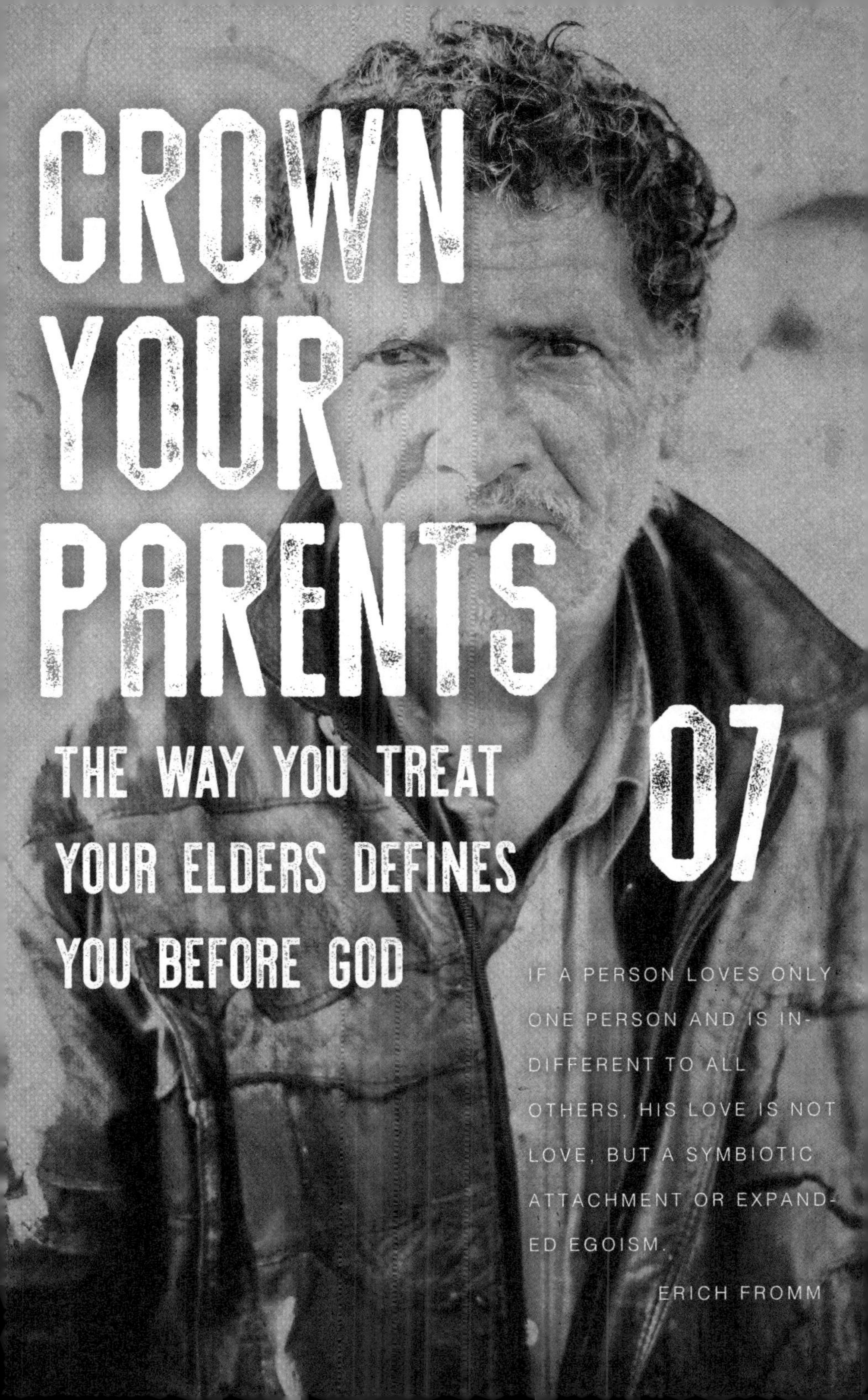

CROWN YOUR PARENTS

THE WAY YOU TREAT YOUR ELDERS DEFINES YOU BEFORE GOD

07

IF A PERSON LOVES ONLY ONE PERSON AND IS IN-DIFFERENT TO ALL OTHERS, HIS LOVE IS NOT LOVE, BUT A SYMBIOTIC ATTACHMENT OR EXPAND-ED EGOISM.

ERICH FROMM

Near the cross of Jesus stood his mother, his mother's sister, Mary the wife of Clopas, and Mary Magdalene. When Jesus saw his mother there, and the disciple whom he loved standing nearby, he said to her, "Woman, here is your son," and to the disciple, "Here is your mother." From that time on, this disciple took her into his home.

John 19:25–27

What a moving scene. It's like that little detail in the middle of the plot of a movie that opens a parenthesis in the storyline to reveal something about the relationship between the characters. Somehow, it touches the sensitive strings of the heart and manages to bring tears to your eyes.

I admit, I'm a bit of a crybaby. I cry in those scenes where the heroes, before performing an act that puts their lives at risk, express their deepest feelings to their loved ones. They really move me. The words of affection the hero expresses before their sacrifice and the way they say goodbye to those important to them are truly touching. They remind us that saving the world is important because our loved ones reside in it. Just for that reason.

I'm not sure if I'll find the right words to describe what was happening in this scene at the foot of that cross. Jesus, the greatest king in history, was fighting the final battle against the power of Hades. On that cross, a conflict of immense proportions was taking place: the rescue of humanity from the clutches of death.

And there he was, the wounded hero, nailed to the cross, his wounds oozing blood into the mud. Bruised, cut, and bleeding, enduring an intense pain from the tearing of the nails, Jesus struggled to breathe. Being hung on the cross, with twelve-centimeter-long nails piercing his heels and wrists to hold him in place by, made breathing extremely difficult. Each breath required putting pressure on the nails, which crushed the nerves in his feet and hands. Inhaling even a little bit of air caused excruciating pain.

With every slight movement, the pain spread throughout his body like a surge of electricity, passing through his arm to his spinal cord, like lightning bolts coursing through Jesus' body.

Every effort to breathe was exhausting for the hero. And then suddenly, he did something unexpected: he spoke to his mother.

Jesus opened a parenthesis in his struggle against evil. Before his final sacrifice, he dedicated some words to his mother, who stood at the foot of the cross suffering as only a mother suffers when witnessing the pain of her child.

When Jesus saw his mother and next to her the disciple whom he loved, he said to his mother:

"Woman, here is your son."
Then he said to the disciple:
"Here is your mother."
John 19:26-27

What was Jesus doing?

While resolving the great problem of sin on the cross, his still found time to address the issue of caring for his mother. During that time period, the responsibility of taking care of parents as they grew older, fell sick, or could no longer care for themselves, rested on their children.

FOR GOD, HONORING PARENTS IS A PRIORITY.

Typically, the firstborn assumed the primary responsibility for the support and protection of their parents. In an honor-based culture like the Hebrew culture, failing to do so was considered an act of dishonor that society condemned.

We know that Mary was a widow, and at that moment, she was about to lose her firstborn, leaving her in a vulnerable situation, especially considering that the religious system would not offer any assistance or alms to the mother of the dissident.

Moved by deep affection for his mother, Jesus called out to her from the height of the cross and said, "Mother, you will not be left alone. Now my disciple John will be your son." And addressing John, he said, "Take good care of my mother, be responsible for protecting her and meeting her needs." And so it was. In fact, a few years ago, I had the opportunity to visit the ruins of the city of Ephesus, in present-day Turkey, where tradition says that John welcomed Mary in her last years of life.

As he was dying, Jesus took care of his mother's retirement and ensured that she received the necessary care in his absence. He thought of his mother while nailed to the cross, in a situation where most of us would only be thinking of our own pain. This brings tears to my eyes. Jesus, the true model of a son, was not only a perfect Son of God but also a perfect Son of Mary.

CORBAN

As I expressed in the previous chapter I believe that more than any other relationship in our life, our relationship with our parents and how we treat them will test the quality of our love.

For God, honoring parents is a priority. The child who doesn't understand this principle doesn't grasp the heart of God.

If you read the Gospels carefully, you will notice that there are certain things that angered Jesus. True love burns against those things that oppose justice, truth, and mercy, even if they come packaged within the box of religion.

Jesus had no problem relating to tax collectors, lepers, and prostitutes. In fact, he associated so much with socially marginalized people that he was known as the "friend of sinners." But there was one group of people Jesus couldn't stand: the hypocritical religious leaders. One of the things that most angered him about them was a consecration pledge called "Corban." In fact, our Master dedicated one of his most direct sermons to those who practiced it:

"You have a fine way of setting aside the commands of God in order to observe your own traditions For Moses said, 'Honor your father and mother,' and, 'Anyone who curses their father or mother is to be put to death.' But you say that if anyone declares that what might have been used to help their father or mother is Corban (that is, devoted to God)— then you no longer let them do anything for their father or mother. Thus you nullify the word of God by your tradition that you have handed down. And you do many things like that." **Mark 7:9-13**

Indeed, "Corban" was a beautiful consecration pledge where a person could approach the temple and dedicate their belongings to God, saying: "Everything I have, all my wealth and possessions, I consecrate to you. From this moment on, I consider nothing as mine, but everything is yours." Essentially, making "Corban" meant surrendering one's possessions to God.

BOX OF GOD

> **WHOEVER NEGLECTED THE AFFAIRS OF THEIR OWN HOME DID NOT QUALIFY TO ATTEND TO THE AFFAIRS OF GOD'S HOUSE.**

So, what made Jesus furious about such a noble dedication? Many children used it as an excuse to dishonor their parents. As I mentioned, in Hebrew culture, children had the duty to attend to the needs of their parents, especially as they grew older and required financial support. However, the Pharisees taught that if a person declared their possessions as "Corban"—that is, an offering dedicated to God—they were exempt from using those possessions to meet their parents' needs, no matter how desperate their situation was. In reality, the child could still use those possessions until their own death if they wished. Some people used this act of religious devotion as an excuse to evade the responsibility of supporting their parents.

Jesus had a strong reaction to this, saying, "Hypocrites! How dare you say that everything you have is consecrated to God if you do not use it for what is most important to God?"

Jesus rejected the idea that true worship could be divorced from social justice. For him, it was a contradiction to show devotion to God while neglecting one's parents.

In other words, whoever neglected the affairs of their own home did not qualify to attend to the affairs of God's house.

In the Kingdom of God, such a combination does not exist.

Period.

A MATTER OF TRUST

But why is honoring parents so important to God? I suppose there are several possible answers. I believe one of them is that God sees in our attitude toward our parents a reflection of our attitude toward Him. In other words, a person who cannot honor a visible and close authority will find it difficult to honor an invisible authority like God. What I am trying to say is that God knows that if we start by dishonoring our earthly parents, sooner or later we will dishonor Him as well.

Honoring parents is a matter of trust for God. I dare to say that God does not trust a child who disregards their parents. Such love is not trustworthy.

A few years ago, my wife and I left our hometown and moved to the capital city for work reasons. It was a period of intense ministry, and our schedule was packed with work, work, and more work. In the midst of this, my mother called me alarmed and said, "Your father is going through a crisis and says he wants to leave the church."

At first, I didn't want to take it seriously, but my mother was adamant: "Your father needs your help."

After hanging up the phone, I stood there, thinking about what it would mean to attend to my mother's request. I would have to cancel several long-standing ministry commitments to make time to go and be with my father in another city. I tried to prioritize all I had to do, and my father always ended up behind another commitment. After all, I didn't have just any job; my job was preaching the Word of God.

Then, I heard the voice of the Holy Spirit within me, hitting me like a punch in the stomach (because sometimes the truth hurts): "If you are not willing to serve your father, you are not serving Me." I didn't like hearing that, especially considering that my schedule was filled with commitments for His Kingdom. But over time, I came to understand that in His Kingdom, it is more important to minister to your father than to minister to a multitude.

So, that's what I did. I went with my father for a few days to a house in the mountains. It was a time of long walks and conversations. I believe that both of us were healed in a particular way during that time. We were able to reconcile and mend our relationship in that place. Together, we experienced God's love and grace. In hindsight, I am grateful for that time, as it taught me the importance of honoring and serving our parents in the Kingdom of God.

THEY HONOR ME WITH THEIR LIPS, BUT THEIR HEART IS FAR FROM ME

Elders hold a special place in God's heart, but unfortunately, the prevailing dishonor in our generation is also seeping into the structures of our Christian families.

Jesus said to them, and also reminded us: "These people honor me with their lips, but their heart is far from me" (Mark 7:6). In other words, it is possible to have our mouths full of words of admiration toward Jesus and yet have our hearts far from His priorities. We can talk about Jesus, but our hearts may not be moved by what moves Him.

So, Jesus raises the following question for us: What good are our worship services if we forget about our elders?

I've had the opportunity to preach in many churches around the world. In doing so, I've noticed a concerning pattern in many contemporary churches: they lack elders.

Where are our elders? Is there a place for them in our worship services? Or, more importantly, is there a place for them in our self-centered, comfortable, and consumeristic lives?

THE ELDERLY

I read some statistics published by the Spanish Red Cross, a non-profit that devotes a large part of its efforts to attending emergency cases related to the elderly. The statistics stated that seventy percent of the elderly in Spain are lonely. Many of them are hardly visited by their children, and in some cases, they remain confined to their own homes due physical limitations, so their only company for weeks at a time is the television.

The Western world is aging. In my country, many of the elderly I see lived through the last post-war of the last century. They knew scarcity, the almost half-century military dictatorship in Spain, and they lived with barely two pairs of shoes and the same suit for every Sunday.

And yet, those elders were able to raise our parents and, consequently, all of us who are now the driving force of society. It is true that families have changed because our world has changed; children go far away in search of work, becoming uprooted. And the parents stay behind. They become long-distance grandparents who, if lucky, see their grandchildren on occasional trips or through phone photos. Even when their children live nearby, the fast-paced urban work-life makes families see each other much less than before. When these elderly people start losing their independence, who takes care of them? In my country, the most common answer is "professional geriatric services."

When I met my wife, she worked as a nursing assistant in a nursing home. She attended to the basic needs of the elderly, feeding them, bathing, and dressing them. Many of them couldn't go to the bathroom by themselves, so my wife helped them get to the bathroom and then took care of cleaning them afterward. She changed the diapers of those who couldn't get out of bed and helped them with hygiene tasks and moisturized their skin. I admit that when I first saw my wife, I fell in love with her external beauty, but when I learned about what she did for those elderly people, I was captivated by her inner beauty.

The professional assistance these elderly people received was very good, but my wife told me that many of them felt a bit forgotten by their children and longed for a home. I still remember her words: "There is so much wisdom in this place that will go unheard."

I am convinced that the moral greatness of a society is measured by how it treats its elderly. Although we have good geriatric facilities in Europe, we have few homes where grandparents have a place of honor at the table and are embraced by their children, grandchildren, and great-grandchildren until they pass away.

I am aware that sometimes professional help is required to attend to the medical needs of our elders, but I wonder if sometimes we place them in nursing homes because we see them as a burden. I believe we must make an honest evaluation of our motivations:

Can we attend to their needs at home, or do they need professional care?

Do we want to take on the responsibility of caring for them and giving them an old age surrounded by the warmth of their loved ones?

Do we perceive them as an obstacle to maintaining the quality of life we desire?

Let's be clear, caring for our elders can be uncomfortable—but true love is willing to be uncomfortable.

Didn't they feel uncomfortable when giving birth to us, preparing our bottles and meals, cleaning us when we soiled ourselves, and enduring sleepless nights when we were sick?

True love is willing to be uncomfortable because love is not just something we say; it is something we do. "I love you" is sometimes translated as "I prepare your food," at other times as "I listen attentively to you," and also as "I help you put on your shirt."

When we were children, our parents had to tell us who we were, but when they become elderly, we will have to remind them who they are. Caring for them, just as they did for us, is a powerful reminder.

THE WOODEN BOWL

When I see how my generation treats its elders, I often remember fable number 78 from the book *Grimm's Fairy Tales*:

An old grandfather went to live with his son, daughter-in-law, and four-year-old grandson. He was so old that his hands trembled uncontrollably. The grandfather and his family gathered every day to eat, but his trembling hands made it difficult for him to feed himself. The food would fall from the spoon to the floor. When he tried to drink from the glass, he spilled. The couple grew tired of this awkward situation.

"We have to do something about Grandfather," said the son. "He's so clumsy. He spills his drink, makes noise when he eats, and drops food on the floor."

So, the couple decided to place a small table in a corner of the dining room. There, the grandfather would eat alone while the rest of the family dined at the main table. Since the grandfather had broken several plates, they served his food in a wooden bowl. From time to time, they glanced over at the grandfather and saw tears in his sad face as he struggled to feed himself. And yet, the only words the couple directed to him were cold reprimands each time he dropped the spoon or the food.

Meanwhile, the four-year-old child observed everything in silence.

One evening before dinner, the father noticed his son playing with some pieces of wood on the floor. He asked, "What are you doing, son?" With sweetness, the child replied, "Oh, I'm making a bowl for you and another one for Mommy so that when you both are like Grandpa, I can serve you food in them." He smiled and continued with his task.

The child's words struck a chord with his parents. That same night, the husband gently took the grandfather's hand and guided him back to the family table. For the rest of his days, the grandfather occupied a place of honor there with them. And after that point, the couple didn't feel as annoyed when the spoon fell, the milk spilled, or the tablecloth got dirty.

I believe the moral of the story is simple to understand. Someday, all of us will also grow old and be unable to property take care of ourselves. Creating a culture of honor toward our elders in our families today will benefit our own old age tomorrow. The opposite is true as well.

CROWN YOUR PARENTS

Studying the meaning of honor, I came across a definition that has become my favorite: "To honor is to place a crown of recognition upon someone's head."

Love IS FOR **BRAVE**

This definition creates a powerful image in my mind. Honoring my parents is not just about obeying them, respecting them, or taking care of them when they need it. It is about placing a crown of recognition upon their heads for all to see.

Thinking about this precious definition, I recalled the proverb that says: "Grandchildren are the crown of the elderly" (Proverbs 17:6).

Beyond its obvious meaning, this proverb declares that the fruit we produce as children becomes a crown upon our parents' heads. In other words, the way we live our lives, the product of our work and testimony, will place a crown upon our parents' heads, either a crown of thorns or a crown of glory. For better or worse, the fruit of our lives will crown our parents. This crown will either uplift them or shame them.

Children who live their lives irresponsibly, who are known for being lazy, quarrelsome, or problematic, not only affect their own reputation but also place a crown of thorns upon their parents, causing them suffering and embarrassment.

On the other hand, children who live their lives responsibly, who are known for their professional achievements, solid marriages, and moral integrity, not only affect their own reputation but also place a crown of glory upon their parents, honoring them and making them happy.

Honor is not just a private matter; it is a public matter. The way we live is not disconnected from our families; it speaks about our parents to others. The greatest act of honor we can give to our parents is to live in such a way that they can be praised because of us. May their ears hear from the mouths of others: "You raised your child well! You made them an admirable person."

What can uplift a father or a mother more than being praised because of their children?

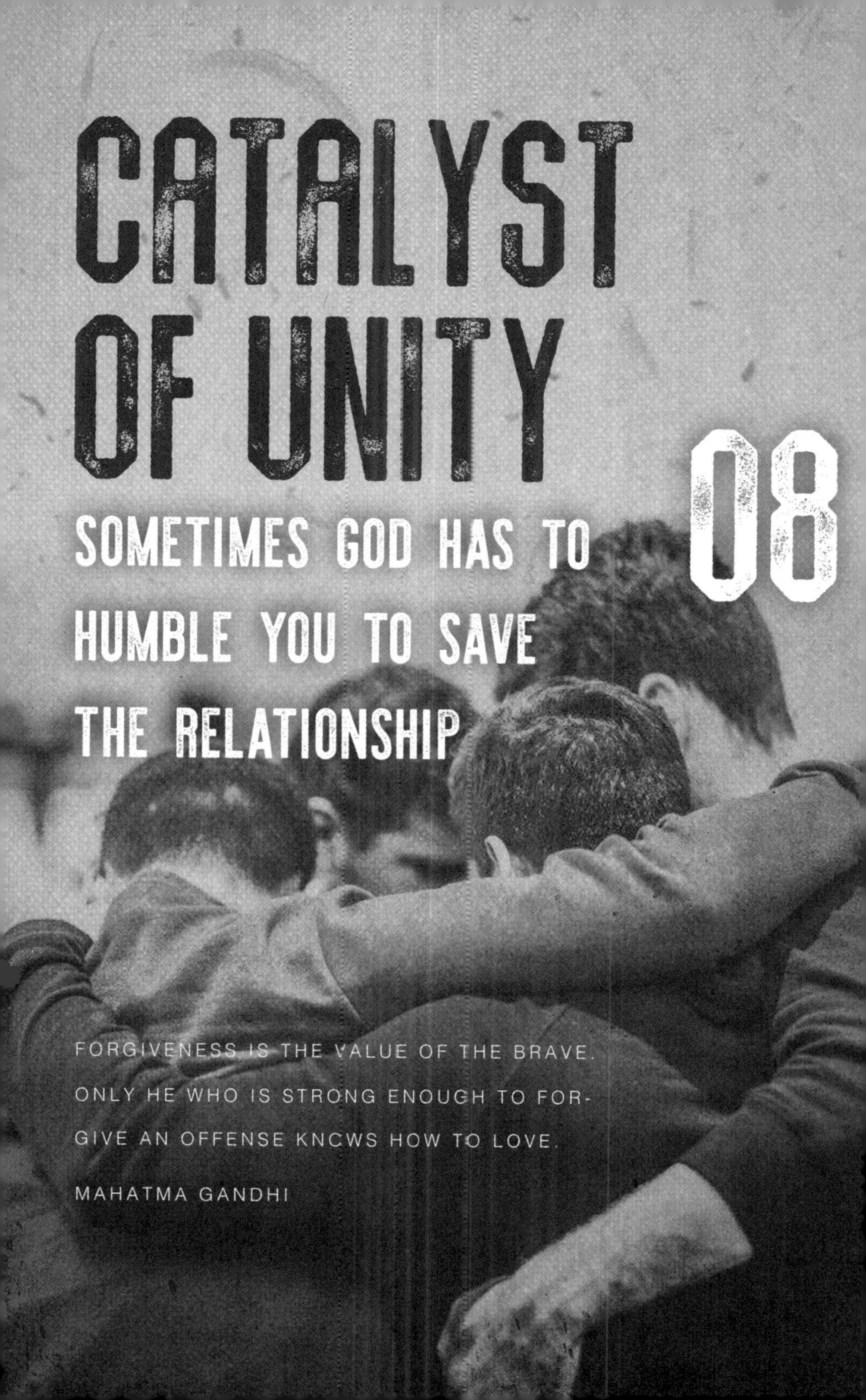

CATALYST OF UNITY

SOMETIMES GOD HAS TO HUMBLE YOU TO SAVE THE RELATIONSHIP

08

FORGIVENESS IS THE VALUE OF THE BRAVE. ONLY HE WHO IS STRONG ENOUGH TO FORGIVE AN OFFENSE KNOWS HOW TO LOVE.

MAHATMA GANDHI

It was just before the Passover Festival. Jesus knew that the hour had come for him to leave this world and go to the Father. Having loved his own who were in the world, he loved them to the end.

The evening meal was in progress, and the devil had already prompted Judas, the son of Simon Iscariot, to betray Jesus. Jesus knew that the Father had put all things under his power, and that he had come from God and was returning to God; so he got up from the meal, took off his outer clothing, and wrapped a towel around his waist. After that, he poured water into a basin and began to wash his disciples' feet, drying them with the towel that was wrapped around him.

He came to Simon Peter, who said to him, "Lord, are you going to wash my feet?"

Jesus replied, "You do not realize now what I am doing, but later you will understand."

"No," said Peter, "you shall never wash my feet." Jesus answered, "Unless I wash you, you have no part with me."

"Then, Lord," Simon Peter replied, "not just my feet but my hands and my head as well!" Jesus answered. "Those who have had a bath need only to wash their feet; their whole body is clean. And you are clean, though not every one of you." For he knew who was going to betray him, and that was why he said not everyone was clean. When he had finished washing their feet, he put on his clothes and returned to his place. "Do you understand what I have done for you?" he asked them. "You call me 'Teacher' and 'Lord,' and rightly so, for that is what I am. Now that I, your Lord and Teacher, have washed your feet, you also should wash one another's feet."

John 13:1–14

That was his last supper with them.

Love is for **BRAVE**

Jesus knew he had only a few hours left before being crucified and presenting Himself before the Father as the ultimate atoning sacrifice. Knowing that context, I imagine Jesus gazing tenderly at his disciples as they sat around the table that night. However, he may soon have begun to recall every absurd argument among them, every competitive attitude, and every offense held in their hearts. Probably, the memory of so many moments when the disciples clashed with each other made him think, "Once I am no longer among them, the team will split." Jesus knew that a group in such conditions would not last long before breaking apart. Too much pride, too much criticism, and too many resentments.

The movement of Jesus in the world was at risk.

So Jesus did something.

Something so provocative that he knew it would leave an indelible memory. Jesus' action was so striking that he was convinced that after witnessing something like this, there would be no excuses for division.

Jesus stood up, took off his teacher's robe, and tied a towel around his waist. Then, he took a basin of water and began to wash his disciples' feet.

I do not exaggerate when I say that what Jesus did was so impactful that they could never forget it. I dare say that this act saved the movement of Jesus. He was able to create a unity among the disciples that seemed impossible.

And he can do it again.

CONTEXT

In the days when Jesus walked the Earth, people did not typically wear closed shoes like we do today, but leather sandals that left much of their feet exposed. It was also common to travel long distances on foot, along dusty roads in the summer and muddy ones in the winter. After a day of walking on dusty roads, through puddles and animal dung, their feet would be in a terrible state. "Dirty" would be an understatement.

When Jews arrived at a house in that time, they would usually have communion with the other members of the family, sitting around a table—a piece of furniture different from what we use today. This table would be raised a few centimeters off the ground; guests gathered around it reclining on cushions or leaning boards. Typically, they lay on the left side of their bodies, leaving their right arm free to eat. In this position, their feet would be close to others' faces, so it was an act of hygiene and mutual respect to wash their feet before coming together at the table to eat.

For this reason, at the entrance of every Jewish house, one could find a basin of water and a towel for everyone to wash their feet before joining the table of communion. In the houses of wealthy people, there were slaves who served the family's needs, and the head of the household would assign the task of foot washing to the lowest-ranking slave. This was a gesture of courtesy to the guests and a convenience for the family. It is important to add that washing someone's feet was considered such a humiliating act that the lowest-ranking slave in the household, the one considered the least responsible and important, had to do it.

This is the cultural context in which the Gospel scene you just read unfolds.

DIRTY FEET

In that last supper with Jesus, there was a group of disciples sitting at the table whose feet were dirty. There was no slave available to wash the feet of the guests. There was, however, a basin, water, and a towel. And yet, none of the disciples offered to do the humiliating task of washing each other's feet.

And then, Jesus did something scandalous.

I'm not using that word by chance; indeed, Jesus' action was a scandal for their minds. Have you ever been in a situation that made you feel secondhand embarrassment? Someone is doing something that shouldn't happen, breaking the protocol or violating social norms. It's so scandalous that you avoid looking. You try to hide your discomfort, but you feel deeply uneasy.

I do not exaggerate when I say that this is exactly what the disciples felt when Jesus got up from the table, took off his teacher's garment, wrapped a towel around his waist, and began to wash the feet of his disciples.

Tension could be felt in the air, and there were uneasy glances among the disciples.

Suddenly, Peter interrupted Jesus and said what everyone was thinking: "A teacher washing the feet of his disciple? That's not the correct order; in fact, it's exactly the opposite. Beloved teacher, you will never wash my feet."

One might think that in the face of such a reasonable statement, Jesus would praise Peter and offer his feet to be washed, adhering to the social order. On the contrary, Jesus looked at Peter and strongly admonished him:

"If I do not wash you, you have no part with me." (John 13:8)

What Jesus was telling him was the following:

"Peter, if I wash your feet, I'll be building a platform on which we can truly commune."

"Peter, if I wash your feet, even though you don't understand it now, it will unite us."

"Peter, if I wash your feet, you will have a part with me, and I will have a part with you."

"Peter, if I wash your feet, we will be one."

Through this act, Jesus was inviting his disciples to become a part of him, because he knew that true unity arises from feeling a part of one another.

And by doing this, he was showing them the only way to stay united:

"If I, your Lord and Teacher, have washed your feet, you also ought to wash one another's feet." (John 13:14)

He was showing them the path to true unity

CATALYST OF UNITY

If there was a difficult group to unite on planet Earth, it was the set of people that Jesus chose as disciples. Jesus brought together in the same team a Jewish nationalist zealot and a tax collector—a functionary of the oppressive empire. He added to his movement both common fishermen and intellectual Pharisees; He had women and men learning together; He even invited masters and slaves to call each other brothers.

If you are not surprised, it's probably because you don't grasp how countercultural it was to create a Church composed of such diverse and opposing people. In that group, there was as much disparity in mindsets, social classes, political stances, and life perspectives as there probably is in your local church. Let's be clear: We are different from the people we have to live with. In your home, at work, or in your church, you encounter people who you find complicated, and coincidentally, they think the same about you. But you can't run away from them; in fact, you know it's important to be together, yet it seems impossible to be truly united.

You are different from the people whom God calls you to genuinely love. Isn't that true? And yet God expects your love to break down the mental barriers that classify everyone into two sections: "them" and "us."

It's possible that you even feel distant from the people you're supposed to feel close to. People who are important in your life, or at least used to be until something happened. Perhaps you live in the same house with a spouse you no longer kiss or have conversations with. You might feel like your children are strangers hiding in their rooms, or your parents are unbearable. It's been a long time since you talked to your brother without arguing. You may have justified this distance with a "we just don't understand

GOD EXPECTS YOUR LOVE TO BREAK DOWN THE MENTAL BARRIERS THAT CLASSIFY EVERYONE INTO TWO SECTIONS: "THEM" AND "US"

each other." The relationship is broken, and you've accepted it. You consider bringing their hearts closer an impossible task.

However, our teacher showed us the way to save a relationship, to unite what is divided, and to restore what is broken.

Jesus didn't wait for unity to arise; Jesus provoked unity. He became the catalyst for an apparently impossible unity.

How did he do it?

By taking a towel and a basin of water and preparing to wash the feet of his disciples.

He taught us that unity doesn't arise; unity is built.

He taught us that unity is not an idea, a speech, or a philosophy; unity is an action.

He taught us that unity is not a document signed with agreements of rights and obligations; unity is a new way of seeing the people around you.

Unity is a change of perspective regarding your companion, your spouse, your father, or your sister. It's about ceasing to look down on them and starting to look up at them while you are on your knees, holding their dirty feet in your hands, ready to wash them.

This is the key to true unity.

There is no other way to make a relationship endure.

In crises.

In differences.

In offenses.

Jesus was showing us the way to unite among ourselves, to keep our heart close to the hearts of others.

When the disciples left that room, they remained different, but they were united. That act changed everything. It changed them all.

The question is, are you willing to be a catalyst for unity in your relationships? True love demands it.

FIRST MOVE: BEND BEFORE THE OTHER

The first move of foot washing is to bend before the other. This represents a position of the heart more than the position of the body. It's about humbling your pride before the other, in favor of unity.

Our pride is the greatest enemy of unity. In fact, my pride almost destroyed the most important relationships in my life.

The Gospel states, "Jesus, knowing that the Father had given all things into his hands, and that he had come from God and was going back to God..." (John 13:3 ESV). In other words, Jesus, knowing who he was, behaved like servant to serve others. This reveals a spiritual principle: He who knows who he is can humble himself. He who knows who he is can and should take the initiative of humility. This means that Jesus was the only one in that room who truly knew who he was.

Jesus knew he was the king of the universe, but he had no problem doing the work of a servant.

Jesus knew the Father had given him all the authority in heaven. Still, he used his hands to clean the dirty feet of his proud disciples.

Jesus knew he was the firstborn of all creation, but he had no problem showing himself as the least among all the brothers.

Why?

Because he knew who he was.

And someone who is sure of who they are does not need to prove anything.

Over time, I have realized how dangerous a person with identity issues can be. When someone is not defined from within, they seek to prove themselves on the outside. Most conflicts I have witnessed in marriages, families, and churches have been the result of the stubbornness of people who wanted to prove something to others.

To prove who's in charge.

To prove who is right.

To prove who is the good one.

To prove, prove, and prove.

And, in the end, the only thing that was proven was their internal insecurity.

I have to admit that my eagerness to prove who is the leader of the house almost destroyed my marriage. Those who know me know that I am very good at debating and often win arguments. Too many times, driven by my pride, I turned a conversation with my wife into a competition. And I won the competition many times! I know how to use the art of manipulation, and I know how to shout and assert myself. But I didn't realize that by winning the argument, I was losing her heart. So many times I thought I was winning a battle when, in reality, I was losing the war. I regret so much the pain that my pride has caused in our marriage.

You can put on the crown of being right and become the king of your kingdom. It's a lonely kingdom where no one but you can stand to be. But I have discovered that in the Kingdom of God, it is more important to have love than to be right. In that Kingdom, the one who loses wins, and the one who humbles oneself is exalted by God.

HUMBLING YOURSELF TO SAVE A RELATIONSHIP

In an atmosphere where people are full of pride, there can be no unity. Unity requires humbling yourself and taking courage.

From my own experience, I believe it's easier to humble yourself in front of a stranger than in front of someone close. When you bow down to a spouse, a child, or a sibling, you put yourself in a vulnerable position.

Think about what that position literal represents. While you have your knees planted on the ground in front of another person, you are vulnerable. How do you defend yourself from that stance? How do you assert yourself? How do you shine?

But don't be mistaken, humbling yourself is not an act of cowardice—it is an act of courage. It takes a lot of confidence, strength of character, and a solid identity to put yourself in that vulnerable position in front of another person, where you literally hand them the power to defeat you. It takes great bravery to renounce your defenses.

Jesus, while being spat on, insulted, and beaten, chose not to defend himself. It may seem that those who tortured Him on the cross had the power, but we know that the real power was with Jesus; if He had only whispered a command to attack, thousands of angels would have come to His defense, annihilating all His enemies.

"Put your sword back in its place," Jesus said to him. "For all who draw the sword will die by the sword. Do you think I cannot call on my Father, and he will at once put at my disposal more than twelve legions of angels?" Matthew 26:52-53

Jesus chose to humble himself, show nothing, and not defend himself He did this to unite us with God. Jesus' humiliation saved our relationship with God.

That's why I believe that Jesus offers you two options to preserve your relationships: either you humble yourself, or God will humble you.

A few years ago, my marriage was suffering because of my pride. We argued a lot over things that really weren't worth fighting over. But that's pride for you; to preserve itself, it doesn't care about destroying the whole world. During those days, I tried to find an excuse to be away from home, and I offered to help a friend with a move. I carried furniture from one place to another, grabbing things with all the rage I had inside me. Suddenly, while trying to lift a dresser from the floor, I heard a bone in my spine crack. At first, it didn't seem like anything serious had happened, but when night came and my body cooled down, I felt the most excruciating pain of my life. It was such a horrible stab that I screamed in bed. I had pinched a nerve in my spine, and the slightest movement, even breathing, caused me excruciating pain. My wife got me out of bed as best she could and, supporting me, took me to the car. She drove to the hospital while I screamed at every turn. When we got there, she told me to wait in the car while she went inside. She came out of the hospital pushing a wheelchair, which she forced me to sit in. I couldn't believe what was happening. Me, in a wheelchair? Over the next week as I recovered, my wife fed me, washed me, and helped me with my needs. I was in a state of absolute dependence. Completely humiliated. But, will you believe me if I tell you that that week was the time of healing for our relationship? When I was humbled, the opportunity to unite our hearts was created. To reconnect.

Sometimes, God has to humble you to save your relationship with another person.

SECOND MOVEMENT: SEEING THE OTHER'S DIRT CORRECTLY

The second movement of foot washing is to see the other's dirt correctly. It's about learning to see your companion's dirty feet without passing judgment on their heart. Giving up criticism is vital to preserving your relationship.

When Jesus saw Peter's dirty feet and prepared to clean them, Peter initially refused. But when he understood that this was the way to remain united with Jesus, Peter said, "Wash me not only my feet, but also my hands and my head." That's when Jesus replied, "You are clean, except for your feet."

In other words, Jesus told him, "Peter, your feet are dirty from the dust of the road, from the mistakes you've made while walking through this life, but you are a clean person." Jesus saw Peter's dirty feet but understood that this dirt did not define who he was. He separated his feet from his heart, his mistakes from his identity.

How different Jesus' perspective is from ours!

Honestly, even though Jesus' blood has cleansed me from all my sins, as I walk through life I feel the dust of my mistakes sticking to my feet. I'm referring to those selfish actions I commit, the half-truths I speak, or the envious thoughts I have. My immature character causes me to fail many times and commit some injustices. These mistakes are like dust clinging to my feet.

But how easy it is to console ourselves by seeing the dirty feet of others, especially those people close to us, who also have dust lodged between their toes.

When Jesus saw Peter's dirty feet, He did not pass judgment on his heart. And yet when we see a flaw in someone else, we often pass judgment on them. We don't say, "Your feet are dirty," but rather, "You are a dirty person." And we distance ourselves from them, feeling justified.

We become expert critics of other people.

Why do we do this? Because it is easier to pass judgment on others than it is to be willing to wash their feet.

I remember a time in my life when I made the mistake of sharing my thoughts about some political issues on social media. I got involved in some controversial debates, and one day I wrote something offensive, something that crossed the line. I didn't want to admit it at that moment, but I had made a mistake in my words.

> **THIS WORLD NEEDS LESS CRITICS AND MORE FOOT WASHERS.**

Then it happened: the debate turned into an attack. My social media started filling up with offensive comments, moral judgments, and harsh criticisms. Many of the messages I received came from people who identified themselves as Christians and felt the duty to publicly correct me with divine judgments. Driven by my pride (and my foolishness), I decided to hold my ground and started defending myself. Everything only got worse.

Among the hundreds of users who were judging me, one person did something different. A good friend called me on the phone and told me he would come to see me in a few hours. To meet me, he had to leave his job and drive several hours to the city where I lived. He invited me to have lunch. While looking into my eyes with an irresistible blend of grace and truth, he said, "Itiel, what you wrote on your social media is like dust on your feet, but it doesn't define who you are. I know your heart, and I know this is a mistake. You are a clean person." When he spoke to me in that way, affirming my identity with such tenderness while pointing out the reasons for my error, separating my mistake from my identity, all my defenses crumbled. I felt like he was not judging my heart;

he was washing my feet. That made me surrender, and I burst into tears. We ended up praying together, I deleted the message, and I asked for forgiveness. I believe he saved me.

This world needs less critics and more foot washers.

THIRD MOVEMENT: POURING GRACE OVER FUTURE MISTAKES

The third movement of foot washing is pouring grace over future mistakes. It's about deciding to forgive someone before they offend you. Making such a determination is crucial for the future of your relationship.

Have you noticed that Jesus washed the feet of disciples who, a few hours later, would use those same feet to run away and abandon Him?

And Jesus knew it.

When Jesus washed the feet of His disciples, He didn't just pour water over them; He poured grace for their future offenses.

Think about it.

FORGIVING WILL BE YOUR ONLY OPTION WHEN SOMEONE OFFENDS YOU.

Jesus washed the feet of Thomas, a man who would doubt His resurrection and divine identity. What does Jesus do with those who doubt Him? He washes their feet, pouring grace.

He even washed the feet of Peter, a man who promised He would never leave Him but, when the test came, denied Him like a coward. What does Jesus do with those who don't keep their promises? He washes their feet, pouring grace.

And, as unreasonable as it may seem, Jesus washed the feet of a man who would betray Him, selling Him to His enemies for a few pieces of silver. What does Jesus do with those who betray Him? He washes their feet, pouring grace.

And then, He let them go.

Choosing to forgive them before they failed Him, pouring grace over them, offering pardon before they offended Him. Jesus' actions brought them back to Himself, with the exception of Judas, who decided to reject the grace offered to him. To forgive like Jesus is to forgive those who never apologized.

If you want to give a future to your relationship, you must decide to pour grace before that person fails you.

That's right: You must make the decision that forgiving will be your only option when they offend you—because, undoubtedly, they will. Consciously or unconsciously, other people will let you down. If you make this decision to forgive today, you won't have to make it tomorrow when you're confused by your hurt feelings.

If your relationship with that other person truly matters, become a catalyst for unity. Set aside your pride, stop judging, and pour grace over the person you love.

FAITHFUL

A LOVE THAT IS NOT FOR SALE

Place me like a seal over your heart, like a seal on your arm; for love is as strong as death, its jealousy unyielding as the grave. It burns like blazing fire, like a mighty flame.

Many waters cannot quench love; rivers cannot sweep it away. If one were to give all the wealth of one's house for love, It would be utterly scorned.

Song of Songs 8:6-7

When you open the Bible right in the middle, you discover this collection of romantic poems that one wouldn't expect to find in a Sacred Book, written in beautiful language with references to nature, but also with a lot of erotic content. The book's constant references to the beauty of the body, the enjoyment of sexuality, and the desperation of lovers are so explicit that Jews were not allowed to read this text until they reached adulthood.

The Song of Songs, or Song of Solomon, is one of the most beautiful works of King Solomon; however, its descriptions raised questions about its presence in the Biblical canon, questions first raised by Jewish scribes and later by the institutionalized Church. In fact, a few centuries ago in Spain, Fray Luis de León's translation of this poem into Spanish led to a four-year prison sentence when he was condemned as a heretic by the Spanish Inquisition.

Currently, the Church's tendency is still to interpret the text as an allegory of the relationship between God and His people, forcing the text too much, moving away from its natural meaning, and elevating it to a mystical place to avoid admitting that God's Spirit could be speaking about what it seems to be speaking about.

Could it be that God is talking about the passion of two young people who want to devour each other with kisses?

Could He talk about the beauty of a naked body?

Could He talk about the touch of skin, the smell of hair, or the taste of lips?

Wait.

Could it be that God is talking about sex?

Although I am convinced that all Scripture speaks of Jesus, including this poem, it is not acceptable to reject this book's most obvious message: the exaltation of romance between a man and a woman.

THE CURTAIN RISES

This great work is composed almost like an opera, and was written to be performed and sung, probably at a Jewish wedding feast.

It is a collection of romantic songs that describe the beauty of love between a peasant girl from Shulam and a shepherd from her region, their fascination with each other, and their passionate sexual encounters.

Although it is not easy to uncover the story behind the poetry, there are scattered verses that, like pieces of a puzzle, come together to form an impressive picture of the Shulammite's faithful love for her beloved shepherd, a love so real that it overcomes the greatest temptation and does not surrender to obstacles.

In reality, this is not a story of two but of three. Of two lovers and a third being who tries to capture the heart of the protagonist.

Although some interpret the story differently, I am convinced that the Song of Solomon is dedicated to the unbreakable love of the Shulammite, who preferred the love of a simple shepherd over the great wealth of the ostentatious King Solomon, who tried to win her over.

One day, the young Shulammite met the shepherd in the field, and the flame of love ignited in their hearts. The Shulammite's brothers, protecting their sister's virginity to later give her to a man who could pay a higher dowry, tried to keep her away from the young shepherd. When she was ready to go with her beloved shepherd, intending that they would contemplate the beauty of the early spring together, her brothers became angry with her and decided to send her to tend the family vineyards far away to keep her away from the boy.

While the Shulammite tended to the vineyards, King Solomon passed through her territory with his royal guard and saw her, captivated by her unusual beauty. He described her as "beautiful as the horses in Pharaoh's chariots" (1:9). Just as Solomon bought the best horses from Egypt, he also wanted to buy the Shulammite. He brought her to his palace and included her in his harem of women; he showered her with gifts and promised to make her queen. All the women in the harem praised the king's virtues and urged the Shulammite to accept this great offer.

Becoming his wife was the opportunity of her life and the payment of the dowry and the social status would benefit her entire family.

However, from the beginning, it was evident that the young woman was in love with the shepherd. She was so in love with him when the women of the harem asked her, "What is so special about your beloved compared to others?" (5:9), she firmly responded, "My beloved is... the finest among ten thousand" (5:10). Several times she confronted Solomon's women, who insisted that she should surrender to the king. "Do not awaken... love until it pleases" (2:7 ESV), she told them. In other words, do not force love to arise. Her heart was reserved for the crownless shepherd.

Even more impressive is reading how the Shulammite repeatedly rejected the king's proposition. "I am my beloved's, and my beloved is mine" (6:3) she said. This resolute rejection was not immediately accepted by Solomon, who persisted with all his courtship efforts. Still, she remained faithful to her beloved shepherd. Her love was so unwavering that Solomon could not do anything but let her go to the mountains to meet her beloved.

MY VINEYARD IS NOT FOR SALE

Toward the end of the book, in chapter 8, the Shulammite makes a defiant statement to King Solomon, who was accustomed to being able to buy anything he wanted. "I am the owner of my vineyard, and I decide to whom I will give it," she said, speaking metaphorically of her sexuality. "Keep your thousand pieces of silver." She then added, "If a man tries to buy love with all his fortune, his offer will be completely rejected."

Not all the glory that King Solomon possessed could convince the young peasant girl to surrender to him. She had already decided to whom she would give herself.

The Shulammite said "no" to the offer of the most powerful man of the moment.

She was the owner of her own vineyard.

Her vineyard could not be bought because her vineyard was not for sale.

Her vineyard had no price because her vineyard was invaluable.

She decided to whom she would willingly give herself.

The man who bought a thousand women could not buy her.

And that made her sexy.

This reminds me of a scene from a somewhat provocative movie. A man enters an exclusive party, where everyone is well-mannered and dressed in formal attire. The man approaches a very elegant woman and discreetly asks her, "Would you sleep with me for a million dollars?" The woman, with a smile, replies, "Sure." A few minutes later, at the same party, the same man approaches the woman again and boldly asks, "Will you sleep with me for a dollar?" Offended, she answers, "What kind of woman do you think I am?!" To which the man responds, "We've already established what kind of woman you are; now we're just negotiating the price."

Today, it is common to hear the saying, "Everyone has a price," to which some proudly respond, "You cannot afford what I am worth." But if your body, your caresses, or your kisses have a price, even if it is a very high price, that is when they actually begin to lose value. If you let it be known that you have a price, you will have to endure others believing they can negotiate with you.

God honored this woman in His sacred book because she did not put a price on her love. Her love was not for sale; it didn't matter what wealth, power, or fame she could gain from the highest bidder.

She did not accept offers. She gave herself to the shepherd as a gift and was not for sale because she no longer belonged to herself.

The text describes this woman in an evocative way:

"My beloved is like a private garden, a closed spring, a sealed fountain. You are a garden fountain, a well of flowing water streaming down from Lebanon... Let my beloved come into his garden and taste its choice fruits." Song of Solomon 4:12-13, 16

SHE WAS A HIDDEN PARADISE ONLY FOR THE EYES OF HER HUSBAND.

She was a private garden, locked with a key that only one man possessed.

She was a hidden paradise only for the eyes of her husband.

She was a spring reserved to satisfy her beloved.

She possessed all kinds of precious fruits and exotic spices that would be tasted only by her lover.

That made her desirable to Solomon.

The value of a treasure lies in its exclusivity.

And although the king had much gold, land, and possessions, that shepherd was richer than the king because he had her. And she had him.

Exclusively.

Perhaps that was the reason why Solomon decided to compose this poem in honor of the Shulammite. Even though Solomon had many women with whom he could have sex, the Shulammite showed him what it means to make love.

FAITHFUL

If there is one adjective that describes the love of the Shulammite, it is "faithful." I don't know if you will agree with me, but I sincerely believe that while this world applauds charisma, beauty, and talent, heaven applauds faithfulness.

One of Jesus' most famous parables describes how a king called his servants and entrusted them with different amounts of money to invest on his behalf during his absence. Some of the servants invested and produced profits for the king, but one of them hid the money in the ground.

When the king returned and called his servants to account, he did not praise the amount of money obtained from their investments; he praised their faithfulness.

"His master replied, 'Well done, good and faithful servant! You have been faithful with a few things; I will put you in charge of many things. Come and share your master's happiness!'" Matthew 25:21

Regardless of the money earned, the king praised the faithfulness of the servants who made an effort to make what their master had given them produce more. They were honored for being faithful with little, and that prompted the king to entrust them with greater responsibilities.

For whoever has will be given more, and they will have an abundance. Whoever does not have, even what they have will be taken from them. Matthew 25:29

This makes me think about Jesus' priorities. This world seeks dazzling people, but Jesus seeks faithful people. People who make a faithful commitment to what God puts in their hands, who take care of it and invest it to produce more, to achieve its full potential. There is nothing more valuable than the hearts of the other people God places in our hands. Faithfulness in our relationships is a priority for God.

When God calls you to love your partner, He doesn't call you to be perfect, He calls you to be faithful.

I remember a comment a friend made about the man she had married: "He's the perfect man. Extremely handsome and the highest earner in his company. If I mention liking something, he surprises me with it when I least expect it. He has me captivated. On Sundays, he brings me breakfast in bed: freshly squeezed orange juice and toast with jam. Every morning, he says goodbye to me with a kiss and an 'I love you' before going to work."

There was only one flaw in this "perfect man": he was unfaithful. What he did for her, he also did with another woman during his supposed business trips. When she discovered his adultery, he no longer seemed so handsome, and his professional success seemed less dazzling. My friend began to hate all his gifts, all his kisses, and all his "I love yous." Why? Because the value of those gestures lay in their exclusivity. When he did the same things with someone else, they lost their value.

Without faithfulness, all other virtues mean nothing. No matter how much you think you have, if you are unfaithful, you have nothing valuable to offer to another person.

That's why unfaithful individuals always fail in their relationships. Their shared kisses taste empty, their shared words sound hollow, and their shared favors seem like penance. And that always raises suspicions. (At least I haven't met an unfaithful person who hasn't been caught).

That's why infidelity hurts so much. It takes all of the meaningful things from a relationship and steals their value, leaving the person feeling cheated.

When we have to account for our lives to Jesus someday, I imagine being faithful to the person he entrusted to us will be a priority. The faithful will be given more, and the unfaithful will have everything taken away from them.

THE LITTLE FOXES

Experience tells me that no one destroys their relationship overnight; it happens over a longer process of neglect.

The poetry of Song of Solomon uses a metaphor to describe how small acts of neglect can gradually undermine a relationship. "The little foxes are ruining the vineyards. Catch them, for the vineyards are in blossom" (Song of Solomon 2:15).

It caught my attention that the author warns that the danger to the vineyards is not from large wild beasts but from the little foxes. Honestly, I needed the help of a farmer to understand this metaphor; logic led me to believe that there is more danger in large predators than in small pests. However, the farmer explained to me that although every vineyard owner fences their vineyards effectively to prevent large beasts from gaining access, but inevitably every fence has some small hole through which the little foxes can enter. The farmer has to make a great effort to detect these holes in the protective fence and seal them as soon as possible.

Furthermore, the farmer explained to me that when a large animal enters a vineyard, it is tall enough to pluck the fruit directly from the vine and devour it. However, the little foxes, being unable to reach the fruit, begin to nibble at the vine's base until it weakens, and the vine ends up bending. They devour the fruit and also disable the vine from producing more fruit in the future. In the end it's the little pests that are a greater danger to the vineyard.

This metaphor reminds us that we shouldn't fear the big beasts, like a major tragedy that devastates a relationship in one fell swoop. While we know stories of marriages that couldn't withstand the death of a child or financial ruin, this metaphor warns us that the most probable danger lies in those little foxes that go unnoticed and gradually wither the relationship, in a slow but devastating process. These little foxes sneak into the relationship through the small neglects of everyday life. That's why the author of the poem shouts: "Catch those little foxes before they ruin the fruit of the vine."

I'll give just one example of these dangerous neglects: ceasing to be grateful for what you have. Before, you admired your partner's virtues and felt privileged to enjoy them, their ability to make a joke out of anything, the conversations that could last for hours into the night, or their unmatched pasta-cooking skills. But what once made you feel grateful now seems boring, and you stop appreciating it.

The fox of apathy enters your relationship; you no longer laugh at your partner's jokes but complain about their flaws; the long face-to-face conversations are replaced by spending time on social media chatting with anyone else, and the pasta, which you once thought was incomparable, doesn't compare to the delicacies others eat.

The lack of gratitude makes room for those little pests that devour the relationship.

UNGRATEFUL

If there's one thing I've learned, it's that infidelity is tied to an attitude of being ungrateful for your partner. You underestimate what you have and think that perhaps you're missing out on something better somewhere else.

When you're not grateful, when you don't feel content, your radar switches on, and you start searching. You look at other vineyards, and it isn't long before something catches your eye.

Infidelity often revolves around a "if only I had that, I would be satisfied" mindset. The idea that you lack something creeps into your mind. You are unfaithful because you can't see what you have. Being ungrateful blinds your soul to all the blessings you have been given.

Infidelity is evidence of an immature and capricious character. It sells an inheritance for an experience, trading faithfulness for opportunity.

Esau, who sold his birthright (a fortune) for a bowl of lentil stew, is a sad example of what you can lose by being ungrateful.

> **INFIDELITY OFTEN REVOLVES AROUND AN "IF ONLY I HAD THAT, I WOULD BE SATISFIED" MINDSET.**

Make sure that no one is immoral or godless like Esau, who traded his birthright as the firstborn son for a single meal. You know that afterward, when he wanted his father's blessing, he was rejected. It was too late for repentance, even though he begged with bitter tears. Hebrews 12:16-17 NLT

The Bible narrates in the book of Genesis that Esau came exhausted and hungry from a long hunting trip, and upon smelling the stew that his brother Jacob was making, he became ravenous for it.

It seems that Jacob knew that when his older brother was hungry, his blood didn't reach his head. Jacob took advantage of the situation and made Esau an offer that any coherent man would have rejected: "Your birthright in exchange for these lentils." But Esau was ungrateful. He was ravenous for the lentils, and he thought that nothing he had could compare to that impressive dish of food. Just like Adam and Eve, who were fascinated with the forbidden tree and thought that nothing in paradise would be as delicious as that fruit. Just like us, who become infatuated with a coworker or someone at the gym and begin to see our partner as less attractive. Soon nothing can compare to having the object of our infatuation

Ravenous and not thinking clearly, Esau made a foolish decision.

He traded his valuable inheritance for something he was going to defecate a few hours later.

FIDELITY IS THE RESULT OF A HEART THAT DAILY CELEBRATES THE BEAUTY OF ITS PARTNER AND PRACTICES CONTENTMENT.

Do you know how the author of Hebrews defines Esau? As "profane"—as "someone who despises sacred things."

When you are ungrateful, you become profane, someone who cannot see the value of what you have, the sacredness of their relationship, who even despises it.

On the contrary, fidelity is the result of a heart that daily celebrates the beauty of its partner and practices contentment.

This is the best way to kill those cursed foxes: By looking at your vineyard and exclaiming to God with gratitude, "This is my vineyard. There are many vineyards in the world, but this one is mine. How precious is the inheritance you have given me!"

Proclaim this even when you don't feel it, because not feeling it doesn't mean it's not true.

"Place me like a seal over your heart, like a seal on your arm; for love is as strong as death, its jealousy unyielding as the grave. It burns like blazing fire, like a mighty flame. Many waters cannot quench love; rivers cannot sweep it away. If one were to give all the wealth of one's house for love, it would be utterly scorned."
Song of Songs 8:6-7

You cannot emphasize one and forget about the rest; all three are necessary for the flame of love to not be extinguished between the two.

But think about all the ways a relationship can cool.

An affair involves two people who have ignited a flame of passion but who lack friendship and comm tment. No matter how much they try to warm themselves with that flame, it is insufficient.

RELATIONSHIPS WERE DESIGNED FOR THE THREE FLAMES TO BURN AS ONE.

It leaves them unsatisfied.

Cold.

One of our friends, speaking honestly about her past promiscuity, told us how cold she felt every weekend when she slept with a man she had just met at the bar: "There we were, two strangers on the bed, acting as if we had a real relationship, but it was a farce, it was empty, and I knew it. There is nothing more unsatisfying than feeling how that man enters your body and penetrates your soul, and when it's all over, knowing that there is no real connection. Looking at him and wondering, 'Who is this to whom I have given something so intimate of myself?'"

Or think about a marriage relationship that has the flame of commitment but has neglected friendship and passion. That flame is not enough to warm the spouses. It leaves them unsatisfied. Cold.

When you separate the flames from each other, you remain unsatisfied.

In a cold darkness.

And believe me, you were not created for that.

THE FABLE OF THE FLAME

This metaphor of the flame reminds me of a fable:

A newlywed couple, frustrated by the constant tensions in their relationship, went to visit an elderly couple they secretly admired.

Love is for **BRAVE**

This elderly couple was known in the village for having formed one of the strongest families in the area. After more than forty years together, overcoming economic crises, enduring illnesses, and raising four children who were already forming their own families, what most impressed people in the village was that they still kissed each other with passion. Although they were not perfect, their love was undoubtedly very much alive.

On the other hand, the young couple felt that their love was dying. First, there were disagreements that led to fights, and as a result of not achieving any resolution, apathy took hold in their relationship. It seemed easier for them to ignore each other and live as single people, even though they were married. And yet they loved each other, so one night they went to the house of the elderly couple in search of the secret to saving their relationship. They were desperate. The elderly couple looked at them lovingly, a look that said, "We have also been there," and told them, "The secret of our successful marriage is hidden in our orchard."

They all looked out the window at the elderly couple's orchard and saw nothing but darkness. It was nighttime; there was not a single lamp lit, and the moon barely illuminated anything with its pale glow, casting shadows among the trees.

The elderly couple lit a candle and gave it to the young couple to go out and search the orchard for a coveted secret. They ventured into the orchard with their small flame, approaching the shadows. But the couple soon became more concerned about keeping the flame alive than finding the secret. Abrupt movements and the night breeze threatened to extinguish the flame, and they didn't want to find themselves unsafe in the wilds of the night. They started walking slowly, shielding the flame and taking care not to lose their source of light. Together, they made a great effort not to be left in the dark.

After fifteen minutes with no apparent success, they returned to the house, feeling sad for not having found the secret to a successful marriage.

The elderly man asked them, "Have you discovered our secret?"

The young couple replied with disappointment, "We have been so focused on keeping the flame alive that we haven't been able to discover the secret."

To which the elderly woman responded, "Actually, you have discovered the secret: working together to keep the flame lit."

This fable reminds me that there is no secret other than this to keep a relationship alive: to fight together to keep the flame burning, to protect it from the winds of the night, and to walk hand in hand through the darkness, trusting in the light of shared love, which is a divine flame.

WHEN A PERSON CANNOT
FIND A DEEP SENSE OF
MEANING, HE BECOMES
DISTRACTED BY PLEASURE.
VIKTOR E. FRANKL

10

SEX

A FIRE CAPABLE OF
MELTING TWO SOULS

Let him kiss me with the kisses of his mouth— for your love is more delightful than wine.

Song of Songs 1:2

I didn't understand it until I read it in the Bible with my own eyes: God likes sex.

I know that just reading this statement makes some prudes' squirm, unable to accept that God has anything to do with sex. That's why I'll write it again slowly, in case your mind needs time to process it:

God

Likes

Sex.

I hope nobody told you something similar to what a religious person told my father when he was a teenager: that sex is the "forbidden fruit." If they did, they lied to you.

God, the poet behind the Song of Songs, is actually inviting us to eat of the "fruit." God sets the table for us and invites us to a banquet full of flavors, smells, and textures.

Like an apple tree among the trees of the forest is my beloved among the young men. I delight to sit in his shade, and his fruit is sweet to my taste. Let him lead me to the banquet hall, and let his banner over me be love. Strengthen me with raisins, refresh me with apples, for I am faint with love. His left arm is under my head, and his right arm embraces me Song of Songs 2:3-6

How beautiful you are and how pleasing, my love, with your delights! Your stature is like that of the palm, and your breasts like clusters of fruit. I said, "I will climb the palm tree; I will take hold of its fruit." May your breasts be like clusters of grapes on the vine, the fragrance of your breath like apples, and your mouth like the best wine. Song of Songs 7:6-9

The divine author uses metaphors to describe the lovers' genitals, taking the form of different fruits—grapes, apples, and raisins—and also likening them to wine, milk, and honey. He even describes them with scents and flavors. It makes you hungry just reading it.

But it doesn't stop there; the poem goes on to beautifully describe the lovers' bodies, likening their eyes to crystal-clear springs, their lips to a scarlet ribbon, their neck to a tower of ivory, their hair to a flock of sheep resting on the mountain, their breasts to two young deer, their navel to a perfect goblet, and their thighs to a carved jewel.

So, what is the purpose of this poem?

To take sex out of the drawer of shameful things and display it in the showcase of honor.

A DIVINE POEM

Although the Song of Songs is a poem with strong erotic content, it is not pornographic. Unlike pornography, the author of the Song seeks to exalt beauty, not merely to arouse. If you take all the descriptions presented in the song, the overall effect is not an excessive fixation on any body part, as is the case in pornography. Rather it celebrates the beauty of the human body as a whole, from head to toe, both male and female. When you finish reading it, you feel more amazed than aroused.

Furthermore, in pornography, sex is the end goal, whereas in the Song of Songs, love is the ultimate aim. And what a love it is! A love that is expressed as fidelity, commitment, and covenant, and finally as passion. It does not detach sex from other expressions of love.

In other words, the Song of Songs is not about how to have sex; it is about how to make love. Still, this poem is controversial for many religious minds. They cannot conceive of romantic encounters between a couple as something spiritual, but that is what they are to God. God is the poet behind the poem.

Acknowledging that this poem is divinely inspired is admitting that God is the God of sex, that sexuality between a man and a woman who love each other is a divine idea, and that these passionate encounters are not only permitted by God but also promoted by Him.

Admitting that God is the mastermind behind this poem is acknowledging that sex is a divine gift to humanity, that God delights when we enjoy pleasure with our partner, and that there is nothing wrong with cherishing our lover's body.

SEXUALITY BETWEEN A MAN AND A WOMAN WHO LOVE EACH OTHER IS A DIVINE IDEA.

But admitting that God speaks through this poem is also admitting that sex was designed to be practiced exclusively by a man and a woman under the covenant of marriage, that sexual pleasure should be connected to committed love, and that faithfulness to our partner is indispensable.

This poem speaks to us about the benefits of sex but also its responsibilities. You should read this poem on your honeymoon. Do it.

SEX IS GOOD

In the romance depicted in the Song of Songs, the sexual encounters of the couple are described as the ultimate expression of their love, reflecting God's view of sex.

From the very beginning of the Bible, from the moment when God commanded Adam and Eve, "Be fruitful and multiply" (Genesis 1:28), it is evident that God is not only the creator of sex but also its main promoter.

Sex was God's idea.

The design of male and female anatomy fitting together was God's idea.

The exchange of fluids was God's idea.

The orgasm was God's idea.

Yes, a great idea.

Some minds may be scandalized by the assertion that God approves of pleasure, but not only does He approve, He deliberately designed the human body to enjoy it.

SEX IS GOOD, AS ITS CREATOR IS GOOD.

Wasn't it God who designed our tongue with taste buds to perceive the thousands of flavors He created for our pleasure? Wasn't it God who designed our body to perceive smells, sounds, and sensations that bring us all kinds of enjoyment? This sensitivity is not merely for survival; it is a lavish display of creativity in our favor, solely to give us pleasure. And this is the same God who designed the glans and clitoris in our bodies with the sole purpose of allowing us to enjoy sexual pleasure. And He declared that it was "very good" (Genesis 1:31).

God is so committed to our pleasure that when He created Adam and Eve, He placed them in a garden known as "Eden," which in Hebrew means "Place of Delights."

If you think that sex is somehow dark, dirty, or bad, then you are implying that its creator is dark, dirty, or bad.

Sex is good, as its creator is good.

And if it is good, we have the responsibility to consider it good and present it as good.

Furthermore, the Church should be the promoter of the best sex.

Sex according to God's design.

Good sex.

The Song of Songs is a challenge to bring sex out of the darkness and expose it to the light of truth.

Not to hide it, but to elevate it to its original position.

THE MANUFACTURER'S MANUAL

A friend told me an unbelievable anecdote that he assured me is true. One of his relatives bought a work truck that, according to the manufacturer's specifications, ran on gasoline. During a financial crisis, the man had the idea to save some money by mixing gasoline with cooking oil. At first, it seemed like everything was working normally, but then the car started smelling like a deep fryer, then it overheated, and the engine was severely damaged. This man wanted to make use of the car's current warranty, but when the dealership's workshop realized what had happened, they refused to cover the repair costs. The man went to the workshop, angry and demanding that they take care of the repair, but they replied, "We do not take responsibility for damages caused by misuse of the car."

Whenever I hear someone say, "I have the right to use my body as I want," or "I choose my sexuality," I imagine God responding, "We do not take responsibility for damages caused by the misuse of sex."

This is the point: if God is the creator of sex, He determines its design. Ignoring the manufacturer's manual can lead to something breaking due to misuse.

God is not the God of prohibitions but of choices.

God does not prohibit sex; He gives you the option to enjoy it according to His design or suffer the consequences of your own choices.

I admit it; I am one of those who still read the manufacturer's instruction manual. Call me strange.

HOW TO CORRUPT SOMETHING GOOD

Sex is one of the expressions designed by God to communicate things to your beloved that you cannot express with words. God created sex not as an end in itself but as a means to express love; in other words, sex is in service to love. When this happens, sex finds its limits in the dictates of love and will not do anything that could offend true love. The theologian St. Augustine of Hippo expressed this by saying, "Love and do what you will," because when you love, everything you desire, including sex, will be for the utmost well-being of the beloved.

However, the purity of sex can be corrupted when it ceases to be a means of expressing love and becomes the ultimate end. The best things in God's creation are corrupted when they stop serving the purposes for which they were designed and end up serving themselves.

For example, eating. I believe eating is one of the most pleasurable activities. However, when it ceases to be a means and becomes the ultimate end, it becomes gluttony.

Eating, drinking, playing, sleeping, or shopping—it doesn't matter what it is. When it ceases to fulfill the function for which it was designed by God, it becomes corrupted.

That is what our lust does with good things: It makes us obsess over something or a sensation, turning a "means" into an "end." It becomes the center of our desires, but in the end, it robs us of the pleasure it once gave.

The word "lust" comes from the Greek term "Epithumia," which combines two concepts: "Epi," which means "in," and "Thumos," which means "mind."

In the mind.

Lust causes something to occupy an excessive amount of space in the mind. Something like sex. Do you know what I mean?

You are driving, in a work meeting, eating, or playing a sport, but you are not really present because your mind is far away, kilometers away, thinking about sex, thinking about how you will achieve your next fix.

Your mind is trapped, because lust equals slavery.

All of your mind is consumed with one thing.

That's how an addiction begins. The worst part, though, is how it ends: It robs you of pleasure.

This was explained to me by a former heroin addict: "When you take the first hit of heroin, you experience an overwhelming pleasure. It's an ecstasy so delightful that you want to experience it again. But the pleasure from the first hit never repeats itself. In fact, the pleasure diminishes with each dose. You need more and more each time, but you feel less and less."

The same thing happens with lust and sex. Pornography, prostitution, or promiscuity are manifestations of lust, evidence that the means have become the end, that sex has ceased to serve love and now serves itself. When sex takes control of the minds of a generation, women are sold on the streets like commodities, intimacy is projected on screens, the innocence of children is abused, and people are stripped with their gaze. When sex takes control of your mind, what they call sexual freedom becomes sexual slavery.

And when you make sex the ultimate end, it leaves you empty, hungry, and unsatisfied. Sex is a cruel master because it was designed to be a servant of love.

SOLOMON SYNDROME

The other day, I saw a chocolate advertising campaign that said, "Pleasure without limits." The slogan is catchy, but what it says is a trap. Pleasure needs limits, or we may end up like Solomon.

At the beginning of his reign in Israel, God appeared to Solomon in a dream and made an unusual proposal: "Ask what you wish me to give you" (1 Kings 3:5). Unlike others who might have asked for power or wealth, Solomon requested wisdom "to govern well... and to discern between good and evil" (1 Kings 3:9). This request pleased God so much that He granted him wisdom surpassing that of any other human, and his name became famous throughout the earth.

If you pay attention to the chronology of Solomon's life, you'll notice he was endowed with unparalleled intelligence. Perhaps the most notable evidence of his wisdom is found in the collection of axioms he wrote in the early years of his reign, known as the "Proverbs of Solomon."

Toward the end of his life, Solomon wrote a strange, somewhat dark and depressing text known as Ecclesiastes. In it, he makes statements like "Vanity of vanities, all is vanity" (Ecclesiastes 1:2). As you read his words, you can sense a certain apathy, as if Solomon had lost the joy of living, as if he had lost his wonder of life's beauty.

Anyone who reads Proverbs and then reads Ecclesiastes realizes that, although they have the same author, the author's mental state was different when writing each book. So, what happened in Solomon's life between Proverbs and Ecclesiastes?

The answer is that Solomon did not set limits on his pleasure. He indulged in all that his body desired, accumulating immeasurable wealth and acquiring anything and everything he wished for—objects, experiences, and even people.

In other words, the wisest man in the world did the most foolish thing in the world: he didn't set limits on his pleasure. In fact, he became famous for having a personal harem of over a thousand women dedicated to providing him with sexual pleasure. This was such an extreme number that I dare say Solomon was addicted to sex. The consequences were terrible—Solomon lost sensitivity, then joy, and finally, he became mentally disturbed.

Excess robs you of your ability to enjoy pleasure. Oversaturation makes you insensitive. It reminds me of a friend who defined himself as a spice addict. Years ago, he started putting spices on his food, initially just on meat. Over time, he ended up putting it on everything, even fruit. Before he realized it, he was carrying his little spice bottle in his pocket to add food at restaurants. I remember his sad confession while we were eating: "I've abused spices so much that I've burned my taste buds. I can't taste anything without spice anymore."

The same thing happens with excess sex. That's why it's so important to respect the limits God has established for enjoying sexual pleasure. If you indulge in pleasure without limits, you lose your ability to enjoy it.

SAFE SEX

I remember another conversation I had with a Christian couple a few weeks before their wedding. At that time, they had a few days off and the opportunity to take a trip together abroad, but they wanted to know my opinion about it. To understand the context, you should know that this couple had the wedding venue reserved, invitations delivered, and they had even agreed on the restaurant menu. The wedding was a sure thing, and we all knew it. The conversation went like this:

"Are you asking me if it's wise to take a trip abroad alone before getting married with the risks that it entails?" I asked them.

"It's a great opportunity that won't come again," they replied almost pleadingly.

"Do you realize that a trip like that involves exposing yourselves to the possibility of having sexual contact before the wedding?" I asked them again in astonishment, knowing that they understood God's design for sex.

To which they replied, "We love each other, we have already decided to get married, and we have everything ready for the ceremony. What's wrong with having sex a few weeks before the wedding?"

At that moment, I sadly reminded them of Solomon's words: "Everything is beautiful in its time" (Ecclesiastes 3:11). When you engage in sex outside the time for which it was designed, it becomes corrupted. Something good, at the wrong time, turns into something bad.

Why? Because sex is something so profound that when misused, it can cause deep harm.

In the sexual act, the deepest union between two people is established. Whether they are aware of it or not, when their bodies unite, their souls fuse together. Paul warned the Church in Corinth, one of the most important trade centers of its time and a city known for the abundance of brothels, about the danger of uniting sexually with a person outside of a marital covenant:

"Do you not know that when a man joins himself to a prostitute, he becomes one body with her, and she with him? For it is said, 'The two will become one flesh'" (1 Corinthians 6:16).

"Becoming one flesh" is a profound statement. Having sexual relations with someone is not a service that you can buy, consume, and forget. Your soul does not forget it because a trace of the other person remains within, even if your mind does not perceive it.

In the sexual act, souls fuse together. Regardless of if it's a one-night passion, whether you know their name, whether they are not there when you wake up, you remain bound.

It is like putting two pieces of metal in contact and subjecting them to the influence of fire. They begin to melt into each other, amalgamating until you can no longer tell where one ends and the other begins. Their fusion is so profound that the atoms of one piece join with the atoms of the other. They change their nature to become something new. Once this union has occurred, attempting to separate the two pieces while cold would result in the breaking of both. Pieces of metal will be lost or adhere to the other piece. They won't return to their original state.

Sexuality is a fire that fuses two souls and turns them into one. It is foolish to think that you can separate them without causing a rupture. Something of him remains in her, and something of her remains in him. Something is lost. Always.

Sex, disconnected from the covenant of love, is inevitably harmful. Some may say, "For us, it was just pleasure and hasn't caused any pain." Sadly, the wounds of the soul are not perceived as quickly as physical wounds, but they are real and more enduring.

For this reason, God established that sex should be reserved for two people who commit to protecting each other's souls forever because in the sexual act, such a deep union is formed that without a protective covenant, it can cause profound destruction.

That protective covenant is called marriage. Practicing sex outside the boundaries of the protective covenant of marriage corrupts the design God gave it: to make two people one.

I remember, during our honeymoon, that when my wife and I made love for the first time, a tear rolled down her cheek. Thinking that maybe I had hurt her, that I hadn't been careful enough, I apologized. But she, looking into my eyes with her soul more exposed than her body, said words I'll never forget: "I'm not crying from pain, but from emotion. I'm amazed by what I feel, although I don't know how to explain it. For the first time, I felt as if someone entered my soul. I feel you closer, deeper, more mine than I've ever felt before. I feel vulnerable like never before, but at the same time, I feel safe."

You don't have the right to enter such a sacred place as someone's soul unless you commit to caring for their soul forever.

Although the Spanish government annually launches advertising campaigns encouraging young people to use condoms in their sexual relations to prevent unwanted pregnancies and sexually transmitted diseases with the slogan, "Practice safe sex, use condoms," in reality, there is no safe sex outside of marriage because a condom cannot protect the soul.

The best sex is experienced when practiced according to its Creator's design: as an expression of love within the covenant of marriage. When this happens, spouses are blessed by God with these words: "Oh, beloved and beloved, eat and drink! Yes, drink to your heart's content!" (Song of Solomon 5:1).

WITHOUT SHAME

There is something that deeply attracts me in the relationship between the Shulammite woman and the shepherd described in the Song of Solomon, something that my soul longs for with. I am longing for that state of absolute freedom.

They stood before each other completely naked yet unashamed, like Adam and Eve. As if that love had created an atmosphere that took them back to paradise, to that place free from turmoil. That place we yearn for due to our exile caused by Sin.

In that time, the man and the woman were naked, but they were not ashamed. Genesis 2:25

I have lived long enough and heard stories from enough people I love to know that some of our most painful memories are connected to our sexuality. I know that my greatest shames have been connected to my sexuality. It seems the same for most.

Someone touched you when you were just a child.

You told them you didn't want to do it, but they forced you.

You gave your body to someone who simply used it.

You're addicted to a type of erotic stimulus that makes you lose control.

You experience intense desires for someone of the same sex.

You buy the intimacy of others online to consume it in secret.

For many, sex is not connected to joy but to sadness; it doesn't resemble paradise but a desert. It's the cause of some of your greatest shames, either because of what was done to you or what you have done through it.

But the Bible recounts that in the beginning, it wasn't like that. We were created free from shame. In a world governed by love, Adam and Eve were naked and felt no shame. Completely naked and completely free from fear. It almost sounds like a utopia, but that's how we were created. However, the rule of love was overthrown by the tyranny of sin, and one of the first things affected was our sexuality.

Because that's what sin does—it corrupts everything.

As soon as they ate from it, they realized they were naked and felt shame. So, they sewed fig leaves together to cover themselves. **Genesis 3:7**

What they had previously seen through the eyes of love, they now saw through the eyes of sin, and they were deeply embarrassed. That's why they covered themselves with fig leaves, to hide from each other's gaze.

They covered themselves with perishable leaves, insufficient, like all our attempts to make our sense of unworthiness disappear. But God loved Adam and Eve so much that He looked upon them with compassion as they hid in shame. He sacrificed an innocent animal, took its skin, and made garments for them to cover their nakedness.

He covered their skin with the skin of an innocent. He covered their ignominy.

The Lord God made tunics of animal skins for Adam and his wife and clothed them. **Genesis 3:21**

But even more astonishing is that God loves you and me so much that He looks upon us with compassion as we hide in shame. On the cross, Jesus the innocent was sacrificed for us to cover our indignity. He was stripped in front of humanity, shamefully exposed before all people, to cover us and free us from the enslaving power of our past mistakes. Jesus allowed His skin to be torn on the cross to clothe us with innocence.

That is the power of Jesus. He takes a cross, which in the time of the Roman Empire was an instrument to condemn the guilty, and turns it into a symbol of freedom for all sinners; He transforms an instrument of shame into a symbol of grace.

Because that's what Jesus does; He restores everything.

He turns our failures into a testimony of forgiveness, liberation, and hope.

For that reason, there is nothing in your sexuality that cannot be redeemed by the power of Jesus.

Jesus can redeem everything that sin has corrupted.

Everything.

Because Jesus is your new skin.

THE BRAVE MAN IS THE ONE WHO
NOT ONLY OVERCOMES HIS ENEMIES,
BUT ALSO HIS PLEASURES.
DEMOCRITUS

LOVE AND DESIRE

11

A TRUE TEST OF LOVE

In the course of time, Amnon, son of David, fell in love with Tamar, the beautiful sister of Absalom, son of David. Amnon became so obsessed with his sister Tamar that he made himself ill. She was a virgin, and it seemed impossible for him to do anything to her.

Now Amnon had an adviser named Jonadab son of Shimeah, David's brother. Jonadab was a very shrewd man. He asked Amnon, "Why do you, the king's son, look so haggard morning after morning? Won't you tell me?"

Amnon said to him, "I'm in love with Tamar, my brother Absalom's sister."

"Go to bed and pretend to be ill," Jonadab said. "When your father comes to see you, say to him, 'I would like my sister Tamar to come and give me something to eat. Let her prepare the food in my sight so I may watch her and then eat it from her hand.'"

So Amnon lay down and pretended to be ill. When the king came to see him, Amnon said to him, "I would like my sister Tamar to come and make some special bread in my sight, so I may eat from her hand."

Then Amnon said to Tamar, "Bring the food here into my bedroom so I may eat from your hand." And Tamar took the bread she had prepared and brought it to her brother Amnon in his bedroom. But when she took it to him to eat, he grabbed her and said, "Come to bed with me, my sister."

"No, my brother!" she said to him. "Don't force me! Such a thing should not be done in Israel! Don't do this wicked thing. What about me? Where could I get rid of my disgrace? And what about you? You would be like one of the wicked fools in Israel. Please speak to the king; he will not keep me from being married to you." But he refused to listen to her, and since he was stronger than she, he raped her.

Then Amnon hated her with intense hatred. In fact, he hated her more than he had loved her. Amnon said to her, "Get up and get out!"

"No!" she said to him. "Sending me away would be a greater wrong than what you have already done to me."

But he refused to listen to her.

2 Samuel 13:1-6, 10-16

This is the account of an obsession that ended in tragedy.

Amnon fell deeply in love with his half-sister Tamar. Both had grown up in the royal palace as children of King David, sharing the same father but having different mothers. At some point, Amnon began to see Tamar differently, not with the tender eyes of a brother, but with the fiery eyes of a man consumed by desire. In fact, it was evident to everyone in the palace that Tamar had ceased to be a girl and had transformed into a captivating woman, dressed in her beautiful princess attire that signaled she was a virgin reserved for the one who would become her husband, the one whom the king would bless.

But Amnon became obsessed with Tamar. He desired to possess her, and the more he contemplated the obstacles that stood in the way, the more his body became plagued by sickness. It became all too evident to one of his friends, Jonadab, to whom he unveiled the secret of his heart. Jonadab concluded by telling Amnon what he hoped to hear: "If you want her, take her." With those words, Jonadab propelled his friend to his death, something none of Amnon's enemies had succeeded in doing.

Amnon devised a simple plan; he feigned illness before the king and requested Tamar's assistance with his care. When he finally managed to be alone with her, he grabbed her hand and declared his desires, saying, "Lie with me because I love you." She resisted, but he persisted. The more she struggled to free herself, the tighter his grip became, causing her arm to ache. Feeling cornered, Tamar implored Amnon, saying, "If you truly love me, ask the king for my hand, for he will not deny you. But do not do this in secrecy, do not act without the king's blessing. Do not commit this wickedness that will bring shame upon me and make you appear foolish." However, instead of listening to her, he gave in to his deep desire to lay with her. He concluded the conversation by saying, "I want you, and I want you now." Forcing her, he pushed her onto the bed, tore her virgin princess attire, and raped her.

He turned his kisses into bites, his caresses into scratches, and his hands into chains. In an instant, he traded the honor of that woman for shame, all for a few moments of pleasure.

For just a few moments of pleasure.

But the most striking aspect of this account is reading how Amnon's emotions transformed in an instant. After abusing her, a radical change occurred in the way he saw Tamar. 2 Samuel 13:15

> **WHEN THE FIRE OF DESIRE WAS CONSUMED, THE ASHES OF CONTEMPT REMAINED.**

When the fire of desire was consumed, the ashes of contempt remained. What he had defined as true love turned into true hatred.

Standing there, gazing at the wall, he began to realize that a moment of pleasure in his body could not compensate for the bitterness that was now invading his soul. She, sitting on the edge of the bed, experiencing intense physical pain that couldn't compare to the agony her soul was enduring, tearfully pleaded with him to take responsibility. As she tried to mend her torn dress, she begged him not to worsen the situation by pretending nothing had happened. Without averting his gaze from the wall, he cast her out of the room like an undesirable.

The woman who had entered as a princess was now expelled as a prostitute.

If you continue reading the biblical account, you'll see that this event triggered a series of catastrophic consequences in their lives and the lives of their loved ones, leaving Tamar deeply ashamed, Amnon brutally murdered, and the family irreparably divided.

An obsession that ended in tragedy.

DOMINATED BY THE SPIRIT OF AMNON

LOVE CONCERNS ITSELF WITH LONG-TERM WELL-BEING; DESIRE ONLY THINKS OF SATISFYING MOMENTARY WHIMS.

This ancient story is a modern story as well. It happens constantly, and you could be the protagonist.

I know you won't like to consider that, but it's the truth.

And the truth hurts, but it also heals.

Our generation is dominated by the spirit of Amnon: we crave love, but we confuse love with desire. Amnon craved love and could feel something intense for Tamar, but he confused love with desire.

He professed his love for her, but it soon became clear that this word held no true meaning for him. It conveyed too much sentiment and insufficient substance. Perhaps Amnon felt the roar of sexual instinct in his gut, the fascination with feminine beauty in his mind, the explosion of infatuation's emotions in his heart, but he did not experience the true meaning of love. He desired her, but he did not love her.

Why do I dare to state this?

Because if he had truly loved her, he would have restrained his sexual desire to avoid dishonoring her.

LOVE OR DESIRE

Someone once asked a wise person, "What's the difference between desiring and loving?"

The wise person responded with this metaphor: "When you desire a flower, you simply pluck it to use for your benefit, but when you love a flower, you water it and protect it, watching over its well-being. If you understand this, you'll comprehend the difference."

To desire is to take possession of someone and expect them to fulfill your needs, regardless of the terrible consequence that they may wither away like a cut flower.

To love is to seek the utmost well-being of another person, even above your own personal well-being. It is to pour yourself onto the beloved like water spilled onto a flower.

So, how can it be love if it doesn't respect the other person?

How can it be love if it shames the other person?

How can it be love if it destroys the other person?

Love concerns itself with long-term well-being; desire only thinks of satisfying momentary whims.

Think of a cut flower—it doesn't wither instantly, but it's already sentenced to die as soon as it is clipped. Similarly, there are many things that may seem harmless, but they actually condemn our partner to death. That's why someone who loves often has to say "No" to themselves or say "No" to their beloved. Someone who loves doesn't seek to make their partner happy for a moment, but to make them happy in the long run.

Sadly, this story reveals that Amnon had more strength in his genitals than in his heart.

He thought that love is measured by how much desire you feel for the other person. He didn't understand that love is measured by how many desires you're willing to sacrifice for the well-being of the other person.

Amnon burned for Tamar with a misguided fire; he desired her, but he never truly loved her.

How short-lived was this man's flame!

He failed to grasp that the fire of desire is a flame that lasts a few seconds, at best a few minutes, but the fire of love is a lasting flame.

I dare to assert that Amnon probably loved the emotions he felt for Tamar more than he loved Tamar herself.

He confused being infatuated with her with truly loving her. He believed that loving is about feeling, when in reality, loving is about seeking the utmost well-being of the other person despite what you feel—sometimes, even against what you feel.

And understand this: You're in danger of being dominated by the spirit of Amnon, whether you're a man or a woman.

TAKE WHAT DOESN'T BELONG TO YOU

Not only did Amnon have no love for the princess, but he also had no fear of the king. The king who was her father and his father. The king who was emotionally invested in his children's lives, but was being insultingly ignored. As if he had nothing to do with their relationship.

Looking at the dramatic picture this history paints, I cannot ignore the symbolic message this story is designed to convey:

We are the sons of the king.

God is the king of history.

The princess we have fallen in love with is also the daughter of the same king.

The king, before being the king, is a father.

The father is emotionally involved in this matter.

And while it can be difficult to consider this, sleeping with the king's daughter without her father's consent is raping his daughter.

This is true if she gives you her consent to do it, even if she insists on doing it: If the father does not give you his blessing you are raping his daughter, because raping means trespassing on land that does not belong to you. And until the father gives her to you, his daughter belongs to him.

When you give free rein to your sexual desire, without the father's blessing, you are desecrating something sacred. Even if you excuse it by claiming it is love, you are putting your hand on the king's daughter.

You must not take what belongs to the king if he has not given it to you.

Do not do it.

And if you do, tell me, how will you defend yourself from the wrath of a king who has been mocked? Or even worse, how will you defend yourself from the wrath of a father whose daughter has been dishonored?

"Calling it Love When You Mean Sex"

It's possible to identify those who possess the spirit of Amnon: they desire pleasure, yet reject responsibility; they pursue physical intimacy, but shy away from the marital covenant; they seek to enjoy the benefits of sex, but refuse to pay the price of commitment.

They excel in emotionally manipulating their partners to achieve their own desires. "Right now, I need you to show me that you love me, to feel that I'm special to you, that you're willing to give me what I ask for without denying me anything," they say, playing the victim. "If you love me, prove it," they declare, as if you owe them something.

But what they're really saying is, "I want sex, now." There's no greater depth to their words than that. It seems like they're talking about love, but they're talking about orgasm.

If no one has told you before, let me shout it to you through these printed words: Sex is not a test of love; it's the reward of love! Offering sex proves nothing, because giving it doesn't require a significant sacrifice. On the other hand, withholding sex until the right time entails the complete sacrifice of our most basic instincts.

The true test of love is being able to master your sexual desires and waiting to have sex until the right moment, when the king gives you his blessing to take his daughter or son. There is no greater proof of love than that.

"How to End Up Hating What You've Desired"

From the story of Amnon and Tamar, we learn that when you satisfy your sexual desire in a forbidden manner, that which you desired so much turns into what you hate the most. Suddenly, his love turned into hatred, and he hated her more than he had ever loved her. 2 Samuel 13:15

It's easy to understand why Tamar would abhor the man who dishonored her, but why did Amnon come to despise her when he had desired her so deeply?

Because he placed an expectation upon her that she could never fulfill. Amnon thought, "If I possess her, then I will feel complete." He believed that having her would fill his life with meaning, and he expected being with her to give him the significance every human soul yearns for. He believed that she was the answer to the deepest questions of his heart: "Who am I? How much am I worth? Why do I exist?"

So, he possessed her, but he didn't gain what he longed for. Emptiness. Without answers. Only an unbearable sensation of being incomplete. The worst thing that can happen to us is to get what we wanted, but then discover that what we truly want was something else.

Amnon looked at Tamar again and felt anger, because unmet expectations always lead to anger. What Amnon didn't understand is that the purpose of his life, the fullness of his soul, the answers to the questions of his heart, were not found in Tamar, but in the King. His father. Our meaning is found in the blessing of the father.

"Dangerously Foolish"

Not recognizing the power that sex holds to create or destroy is the evidence of a foolish generation.

Misused sex can turn love into hatred.

MISUSED SEX CAN TURN LOVE INTO HATRED.

As a pastor, I constantly receive messages from young people who believed that giving sex to their partners before marriage would bring them closer and propel them toward marriage, but they painfully discovered that sex at the wrong time separated them and nullified all their future plans.

Like the email from a fifteen-year-old girl who lamented giving a "proof of love" to someone who ended up hating her: "I had never been with anyone before, but I was madly in love with him. Time passed, and we ended up in bed together, doing things I knew were not right, but I broke my own rules so as not to lose him. That's the biggest mistake I could have made. I believed that by doing what the guy wanted, he would be crazy about me, but that's not true.

Now we're not together anymore, and I feel like he took something from me. I hate him."

There have been many times when I have run after young people who were leaving the church community. As I begged them not to go, they responded with tear-soaked words.

"I can't be near that person I used to love but now hate."

To be honest, the people they referred to with such resentment were not the stereotype of cruel individuals. I wish they were because it would have been easier to lash out against them. These were young people with Christian values who were striving to live according to their beliefs.

Simply put, they were young people dominated by the spirit of Amnon.

They were young people who longed for love but confused love with desire.

They were young people who rushed to take something from the other person that God had not yet given them.

They were foolish, but not cruel.

Quite foolish, if I may be clear, but not wicked. However, one doesn't need to be cruel to create a catastrophe in someone's life, and often ignorance has caused more pain than malice. Just like Tamar, I have seen the lives of many young people ruined by an Amnon who couldn't control his desires, later burdened by an unbearable weight of guilt that ultimately destroyed the relationship and pushed one of them, at times, away from God due to a sharp sense of shame for what occurred.

Believe me, if there's something that should instill fear in you, it's the knowledge that one day you'll stand face to face with the king, accounting for the death of one of his daughters due to the irresponsibility with which you treated her heart. Consider this the next time you're tempted to go too far with a princess.

A TRUE TEST OF LOVE

Do you want to give your partner a true test of love? Don't give them sex on any random night; give them your virginity on your wedding night. I know what I'm saying may be subject to ridicule in a promiscuous culture that places little value on sex and pressures young people to shed their virginity as soon as possible, as if being a virgin were a shameful stigma.

It takes courage to live on a higher level than your desires. But preserving virginity as a proof of love for someone special isn't a mark of shame; it's a badge of valor. Only the brave can conquer themselves.

The promiscuous culture has taught us that freedom is always doing what you desire, satisfying your instincts without restrictions. But there's nothing more enslaving than yielding to the dictates of your desires, becoming a servant of your instincts. It takes courage to live on a higher level than your desires. It takes courage to deny your sexual impulses. Love is for the brave.

Anyone can engage in sex, but only the brave make love. The love of the brave says "No" to certain stimuli to say "Yes" to certain convictions. And believe me, what you gain far surpasses what you lose.

But honestly, as someone who has struggled in the battle against my sexual desires, I asked God: 'Why do we develop our sexual desires before we have your approval to use them?'

By the age of fourteen, most men and women are physically ready for sexual relations and have the impulse to engage in them. We are a boiling pot of hormones. However, God doesn't permit us to have sexual relations with our partner until marriage, which often doesn't happen for many years.

Wouldn't it be easier if our sexual awakening happened on our wedding day? Why has God designed us in such a way that we have to fiercely fight against our sexual desires to arrive at marriage as virgins?

God's answer gave purpose to my sexual struggle: "By activating your sexual desire before you have permission to use it, I am giving you the opportunity to bring the treasure of your conquest to your beloved on your wedding night."

In ancient times, when a soldier conquered a city, he had the right to take a portion of its treasure to present as a gift to his beloved, honoring her for faithfully waiting for him at home.

The significance of that treasure wasn't its quantitative value, but its symbolic worth. The more challenging the battle to conquer that city had been, the greater value the treasure held. This object would be displayed in the home as a memento for the family of his bravery in battle.

God allows you to experience sexual desire before you have the approval to use it so you have the opportunity to conquer yourself and win the battle against your sexual desires in order to bring something valuable to your beloved on your wedding night. A gift for which you had to wage a war against yourself, the great treasure of your personal conquest, your virginity.

Anyone can give an expensive item to another person if they have enough money. However, only the brave who have conquered their sexuality can give their virginity to the person they love, something that money could never buy it.

On my wedding night, I gave something exclusive to my beloved, something I haven't given to anyone else and never will. A treasure that cost me a great struggle to attain, representing years of waiting, discipline, and sacrifice. It also represented cold showers, desperate escapes, and pleas for help. And, let's admit it, it represented resisting the mockery of others for years. It represented a story of valor, it was a gift of invaluable cost. I'm talking about my virginity.

That night, like a brave warrior, I entered my home, I entered her. I carried with me my special treasure, ready to give it to her and only her. With tears of joy, I said to her:

"With this treasure that I now give you, I want to declare that you are worth to me all the sacrifice it took to bring you my virginity on this night. That is what you're worth to me, all this sacrifice, this entire story of personal conquest. My story."

That was my test of love.

Can any random night of desire surpass a night of love like this?

THE GOD WHO BENDS AND LIFTS US FROM THE DUST

If you gave your virginity to someone who is no longer a part of your life and you think, "There is no restoration for my mistake; I have nothing exclusive to offer the person I will marry. I have lost it, and it's irreplaceable," let me tell you that our God is capable of restoring everything, even your sexual purity. God's grace has the power to make all things new, even to give you a new purity, so you can fight for it and bring the treasure of your conquest to someone special on your wedding night.

Because virginity is a matter of the soul more than the body, and there is no better soul restorer than Jesus.

The Gospel tells us the story of a woman whose soul was ruined, in the dust.

Then the scribes and the Pharisees brought a woman who had been caught in adultery. They made her stand in the middle and said to Jesus, "Teacher, this woman was caught in the very act of committing adultery. Now in the law, Moses commanded us to stone such women. So what do you say?" John 8:3-5

Can you imagine the shame this woman was feeling?

Caught in the act of adultery.

Abandoned by the man she had lain with.

Violently brought by her accusers to the temple.

Exposed before a crowd with stones in their hands.

Aware that she was guilty of succumbing to her destructive desires.

Thrown in the dust.

I can imagine her lying on the ground, dirty and semi-naked. Her dress was torn by the destructive power of desire. Like Tamar's.

"The Law says she should be stoned, but what do you say, Jesus?"

Grace is about to pass judgment.

Because grace is a person, grace is Jesus.

Jesus bent down and started writing on the ground with his finger. John 8:6

Silently, grace bent down to her level.

To the level of the dust.

And with his finger, he drew in the dust.

The first time God bent down and put His hand in the mud for us was when He formed the human being from the dust of the earth. Perhaps, as He bent down again next to this woman and touched the dust, He was remembering where He came from, reminding Himself and reminding us of where we come from. We are clay; without the spirit of God, we are nothing more than dust carried by the wind.

The Law stood upright with a stone in hand.

Grace bent down and put His hand in the dust.

Between the accusers and the adulterous woman stood Jesus, diverting the gazes that were fixed on the ashamed woman toward Him, absorbing all the anger that the crowd felt toward this sinner onto Himself.

Jesus was willing to die to create something new in her.

And indeed, He did so on a cross later.

We don't know what Jesus wrote on the ground; perhaps He wrote the commandments. But as the accusers persisted in demanding a resolution, Jesus stood up, head held high, challenging the accusers. Pointing to the dust, He said:

"Let any one of you who is without sin be the first to throw a stone at her." John 8:7

The accusers, accused by their own consciences, silently admitted that they too were guilty of breaking God's commandments and began to leave one by one.

When the two of them were alone, Jesus bent down again, but this time to lift the woman from the dust. To restore her soul, to make her new. Then He straightened up and asked her:

"Woman, where are they? Has no one condemned you?"

"No one, sir," she replied.

"Neither do I condemn you," Jesus declared. "Go now and leave your life of sin." John 8:10-11

In this way, He transformed an adulteress into a virgin.

He made her new, gave her a fresh start.

That is the power of grace.

Similarly, Jesus bends down toward you, to the level of the dust where you currently stand, and asks, "Where are those who accuse you?" He refers to those voices outside or inside you that condemn you, saying:

Your mistake is irreparable.

There's no more purity in you.

You have nothing to offer.

Jesus lifts you from the dust to make you new and reminds you:

"The only voice you should listen to is mine, and today I tell you: I do not condemn you; go and sin no more."

Many, when reading these words, mistakenly believe that Jesus was giving a warning to the woman in the style of, "I have forgiven you, but be careful not to go back to your old ways." But it's not like that at all. Jesus was empowering her with those words of grace so that she would never sin again. That's what grace does—it not only lifts you from the dust but empowers you to stand upright for the rest of your life.

Therefore, when you arrive in heaven, if you want to personally meet that woman, don't even think about referring to her as "the adulterous woman." In heaven, she is known as "the woman who was forgiven and never sinned again."

Because grace gives you a new name.

In a single moment, the one who started reading this chapter as an adulteress can finish it as a virgin. Someone whose dress was torn by the destructive power of desire can receive a new garment of purity.

That is the restoring power of grace.

REDEEMERS

THE RESTORATION OF THE PEOPLE

12

I KNOW OF NO OTHER
SIGN OF SUPERIORITY
THAN KINDNESS.

LUDVIG VAN BEETHOVEN

When the Lord began to speak through Hosea, the Lord said to him, "Go, marry a promiscuous woman and have children with her, for like an adulterous wife this land is guilty of unfaithfulness to the Lord." So he married Gomer, daughter of Diblaim, and she conceived and bore him a son.

The Lord said to me, "Go, show your love to your wife again, though she is loved by another man and is an adulteress. Love her as the Lord loves the Israelites, though they turn to other gods and love the sacred raisin cakes."

So I bought her for fifteen shekels of silver and about a homer and a lethek of barley. Then I told her, "You are to live with me many days; you must not be a prostitute or be intimate with any man, and I will behave the same way toward you."

Hosea 1:2-3, 3:1-3

When this passage takes place, it was a challenging time to be a prophet. The people had forsaken their loyalty to the true God to give their affections to false gods. Even though Hosea had confronted the people's unfaithfulness with fervent speeches, there were no words capable of thawing their icy hearts.

Then, God spoke to His prophet and told him something that still echoes in eternity: "From now on, you will be my living message, embodying my love for this unfaithful people, and you will feel everything I feel."

God asked Hosea to turn his life into a sort of living representation of His relationship with Israel, almost like a prophetic performance. He asked Hosea to love a woman who was beautiful, but who also had serious emotional problems. He asked him to love a promiscuous woman who would be unfaithful to him. He asked him to persist in loving her despite her betrayals.

What you can read on those pages is the challenge that God presents to Hosea—to love as He loves.

GOD HAS A HEART

This prophetic book is gripping because it reveals an aspect of God's nature that we are not accustomed to perceiving: His vulnerability. As you read this book, you get the sense that God is baring Himself and his feelings, as if He is opening His chest before us and showing us the depths of His being. By exposing Himself in this way, we then can discover something fascinating, something that many may not have suspected: that God has a heart, and that heart can ache.

"My heart is torn within me." Hosea 11:8

As surprising as it may be, the Bible states that God—the Creator, the Eternal, the Almighty, the Omniscient, the Holy One, and a myriad of other divine attributes—has a heart. Clearly, this is an anthropomorphism, which means attributing human characteristics to something that isn't human, in this case a divine being. We know that God is spirit, without physical form or gender. However, when the Bible says God has a heart, it is a metaphor that describes a divine reality in words understandable to us.

A God with a heart is a God who feels, responds, and experiences; in other words, He is vulnerable to external stimuli. The book of Hosea presents to us a God capable of suffering. And what is the cause of His suffering? People.

People, like you and me, whom God created to love and endowed with the attribute that makes a true relationship possible: the freedom to choose whether or not to respond to His love. The freedom to do as we please with His heart, even to break it.

As I write these words, I recall the sound of a friend's crying when her husband was unfaithful. It's unforgettable. There are many different ways to weep, and on that day, as my wife and I held her tight, her tears flowed from a heart shattered by the person she had given it to at the altar.

Reading the book of Hosea, I have the sense of hearing the same sound, as if it were not written with ink, but with the tears of a betrayed lover. Almost at the beginning of the Bible, when it describes how the human beings God created to love used their freedom to betray Him and destroy His creation, the author describes what happened at the very center of divinity:

"Then the Lord regretted that He had made human beings on the earth, and His heart was deeply troubled." Genesis 6:6 NTV

Other translations express it by saying, "His heart was pained within Him," as if His heart was being torn apart.

God's heart was broken! It was the people He took the risk to love, the ones to whom He gave power over His heart, who took that precious gift and shattered it. Perhaps the drops that fell from the sky during the flood were the tears of a God with a broken heart.

THE STORY FOUND IN THE BIBLE IS THAT OF A BEING WHO LOVES AND CONTINUES TO LOVE EVEN WHEN IT IS NOT RECIPROCATED.

What does this say about God?

Perhaps for some this is a new perspective. We are so accustomed to imagining divinity as an impersonal force or as a set of laws governing the cosmos that it's difficult to picture the divine as an emotional being. It's easy for us to perceive of God as a creator, a supreme judge, a collection of truths, a religious system...but as a lover? As someone who takes the risk of making a declaration of love to beings with free will?

As someone who becomes vulnerable to the pain of possible rejection from the ones He loves? This is a deeply challenging view for all of us who call ourselves His followers.

Contemplating this makes me reconsider what the Bible is really about, what the central theme of this cosmic drama is. Is the Bible the owner's manual?

In reality, the story found in the Bible is about a being who loves and continues to love even when it is not reciprocated. When I fix my gaze on Jesus nailed to that cross, the Almighty wrapped in delicate human flesh and exposed before all, all I can think of is that it's the most grandiose declaration of love ever made. Jesus is the heart that God offers to the world, a heart that was crushed on that cross, yet persisted in loving us.

And what does His story teach us about what it truly means to love? It teaches us that to love is to make yourself vulnerable by exposing your feelings first, even at the risk of them not being reciprocated. To love is to empower the other to say either yes or no, and to deeply affect your emotions. To love is to take the risk of having your heart crushed.

SURELY

Surely Hosea must have been greatly surprised by the strange commission from his Lord, but he obeyed. He married Gomer, a beautiful woman with a hidden weakness for jewelry, clothes, and luxuries.

At first, the marriage seemed to work perfectly; they even had two children. However, over time, the hidden ambition in Gomer's soul began to surface. She was dissatisfied with what Hosea was able to provide. Instead of dedicating more time to business to improve their lifestyle, he spent hours praying to his God and preaching the divine message. Gomer began to disconnect her soul from her husband and look at other men, wealthy men. Other men who, in her view, could quench her soul's thirst. In truth, she was thirsty for something she couldn't quite identify, but she believed that with a few indulgences, new shoes, or perhaps some earrings, she would be satisfied.

Despite having had two pregnancies, Gomer maintained an attractive figure and a beautiful face that tended to capture the hearts of lustful men. Driven by her want for more, she turned to these other men. At first, they were single men who rewarded her with a dress, a jewel, or other luxury items after sleeping with her. But Gomer's thirst eventually led her to sleep with married men who paid her handsomely for her silence. For a few months, she managed to hide her double life, but then something happened that she couldn't hide: She became pregnant by another man, although she wasn't even sure who the father was. Hosea suspected that what his God had told him years ago was coming true. His wife had avoided sleeping with him for months, and their sexual encounters had been rare. Still, she insisted that the baby was Hosea's. After giving birth, Gomer decided she didn't want to spend her life as the wife of a poor prophet or the mother of demanding children. So, taking all her accumulated wealth, she abandoned her family, leaving a note on the bed that said:

"I am thirsty for something you cannot give me. I deserve a better life than this, and I will go out and search for it until I am satisfied."

At this point in the story, it would be easy to place ourselves on a platform of superiority and judge Gomer for her actions. But are we better than her? I believe not. At least, I have found myself many times under the influence of what I call the "Gomer Syndrome." To me this means having a deep thirst in your soul for something that makes you feel complete, and seeking satisfaction in the wrong places. In other words, the Gomer Syndrome means trying to quench your thirst with the wrong water. Most of us tell ourselves that the reason we are constantly unsatisfied is simply because we haven't been able to take a good sip yet of whatever we think we're looking for. In this way, we continue desperately seeking more water elsewhere. Like Gomer, we might even sell important things for a sip that promises the satisfaction our thirsty soul longs for.

The Gomer Syndrome reminds me of a conversation Jesus had with a deeply thirsty woman at a well in the city of Samaria under the scorching sun of Israel. This woman must have been as attractive as Gomer since she had a history of five husbands, but undoubtedly, she had serious emotional issues.

This conversation reveals the only source capable of satisfying the human soul.

When a Samaritan woman came to draw water, Jesus said to her, "Will you give me a drink?" (His disciples had gone into the town to buy food.)

Love is for **BRAVE**

The Samaritan woman said to him, "You are a Jew and I am a Samaritan woman. How can you ask me for a drink?" (For Jews do not associate with Samaritans.)

Jesus answered her, "If you knew the gift of God and who it is that asks you for a drink, you would have asked him and he would have given you living water."

Jesus answered, "Everyone who drinks this water will be thirsty again, but whoever drinks the water I give them will never thirst. Indeed, the water I give them will become in them a spring of water welling up to eternal life."

The woman said to him, "Sir, give me this water so that I won't get thirsty and have to keep coming here to draw water."

He told her, "Go, call your husband and come back."

"I have no husband," she replied.

Jesus said to her, "You are right when you say you have no husband. The fact is, you have had five husbands, and the man you now have is not your husband. What you have just said is quite true."

"Sir," the woman said, "I can see that you are a prophet. John 4:7-10, 13-19

The Gospel presents this scene by saying that Jesus and the Samaritan woman were alone at the well. Then Jesus makes a very provocative request: "Give me a drink." It's easy to miss the impact of this conversation without understanding the Hebrew culture of that time. In that culture, if a man approached a strange woman in a private conversation with these words, it could be understood as a proposition for a sexual encounter. "Drinking from a woman's water" was a Hebrew euphemism (widely used in proverbs) for having sexual relations with her.

Undoubtedly, it wasn't the first time a strange man had made a similar proposition, as she had a well-known history in the city of promiscuity. However, Jesus didn't actually want to drink the woman's water; He wanted to offer her Living Water that would satisfy her soul for all eternity.

But why does Jesus start the conversation in such a provocative way? Because Jesus knows that the quickest way to a person's heart is through a wound. And this question directly addressed the wound of that woman.

Quickly, Jesus connects the dots in the conversation, linking the woman's thirst with her history of promiscuity. Jesus tells her, "You've tried to quench your thirst with the love of men and have gone from one man's bed to another, only to discover that you're still thirsty. This is because your soul longs for a kind of love that can't be obtained from any man; your soul has been designed to be completed by the love of God. That divine love is the only source capable of satisfying you eternally."

Just like Gomer and the Samaritan woman, we can use romantic relationships as sources to quench the thirst of our souls—but if we do this, we'll remain unsatisfied. We'll risk using people's affection to momentarily appease our thirst, eventually draining them completely and in the end, only resenting them for not satisfying us.

We can do this over and over, desperately absorbing any drop of love that someone offers us. Eventually, like addicts, we're willing to give up anything for our daily fix, capable of destroying even beautiful things for one more drop. But tomorrow, we'll be thirsty again.

THE AUCTION

Returning to the story of Hosea, we're not certain how long Gomer had been selling her body for money, but what we do know is that the woman who began as a high-priced prostitute ended up a harlot despised by her clients.

Perhaps, Gomer aged, fell ill, or simply lost her appeal to men, and the woman who had once been highly sought after now begged men for a service that would allow her to cover her expenses. Gomer's debt kept growing until the situation became unbearable, and her creditors took possession of her. She literally became a slave, owned by the very thing she thought she possessed.

At some point, news reached Hosea that this woman who was still legally his wife was going to be auctioned as a slave in the market of a neighboring city. With a broken heart and a whirlwind of emotions, the prophet didn't know what to do: Should he leave her to her fate? After all, she was receiving a just punishment.

Confused, he cried out to God, laying his case before Him, and he received an answer: "Hosea, do you remember that years ago I told you that you would be my living message, that you would embody my love for this unfaithful people and feel everything I feel? Now, love this woman, pay her debt, and bring her back to you so that Israel may understand the true meaning of love."

I dare not claim that obeying the voice of God was an easy decision, but what I do know is that when someone responds to the challenge of love, the divine Spirit empowers them to do what seems humanly impossible. I have no doubt about that.

So, Hosea went to the slave market and stood at a distance, watching as Gomer was brought in and placed on the auction block.

There was his wife, stripped of her clothes, completely naked before the crowd. That human misery was nothing but the shadow of the lovely young girl he had kissed on their wedding day, no longer beautiful. The auctioneer pointed at her with a stick, instructed her to open her mouth to display her teeth, as is done with livestock to demonstrate their health, and then the bidding began.

"Who offers five silver coins for this slave?" shouted the auctioneer. The crowd ignored him. "Does anyone offer five silver coins? Anybody?"

The buyers showed no interest whatsoever until someone shouted:

"I'll buy her for one silver coin!"

"One silver coin is too little. Who offers two?" The auctioneer attempted to encourage potential buyers.

"I'll buy her for one silver coin!" the one who seemed interested in her insisted. "A silver coin is the worth of a woman in such conditions."

"One silver coin going once," began the auctioneer, counting the bids, "one silver coin going twice," he continued. And then suddenly, the voice of true love shattered the silence.

"I offer fifteen silver coins, five baskets of barley, and a measure of wine!" Hosea shouted,. Shocked, everyone fell silent.

"But that woman isn't worth what you're offering for her," the surprised seller exclaimed.

"I'm giving everything I have, because that's what she's worth to me."

And covering her nakedness with a sheet, Hosea took Gomer into his arms and carried her back home. As he walked away from the crowd, he cried out to the people:

"Hear, O Israel, poor slave of the idols to whom you've given your heart! This is how your God loves you!"

REDEEMERS

The Bible uses a powerful word to describe what Hosea did for Gomer: "redemption."

If you've read the Bible, you may have noticed that this word appears several times to refer to what Jesus did for us on the cross.

"Redemption" is a word that emerged in an infernal atmosphere, within the slave markets of empires, where men, women, and children were displayed as if they were things to be bought, degraded as if they were animals. This word represents bringing something from heaven into the very center of hell, because to redeem means to free a person from slavery by paying a price. When someone redeemed a slave, they took on that slave's debt and set them free.

Not only that, but they also restored their lost dignity. I would dare to say that a redeemer is someone who causes heaven to invade the life of another person, someone whose reality could be considered a genuine hell. A redeemer is someone who fights against the forces that destroy and commits to being a restorer of lives broken by sin.

That's what Hosea did for Gomer, and wasn't that what Jesus did for us on the cross? Gomer had become indebted because of her mistakes, a slave to her passions, but Hosea was willing to pay the price to bring her back home. He entered the depths of hell to set her free, daring to be a bearer of heaven over a ruined life. Hosea's actions represent a redeeming love, a love that is willing to pay the price to bring the other back into a relationship. A love that restores the lost dignity of another.

And that's exactly what God challenges us with through the example of the prophet Hosea.

What do you do when a relationship is turning into a hell?

When offenses pile up?

When complaints gain ground, words sound like screams, and looks represent reproaches?

What do you do when debts in a relationship accumulate and you are on the verge of becoming slaves to your passions?

OUR WAY OF TREATING WHAT IS CREATED REFLECTS OUR FEELINGS TOWARD ITS CREATOR.

You can let hell take control, or you can attack it with the forces of heaven, with forgiveness, honor, patience, compassion, actions that make the forces of evil tremble. You can become a redeemer. You can pay the price for your partner's debts and free them from any demands. You can pay the price to bring them back and forgive their mistakes.

Why should we pay the price for someone else?

Because our way of treating what is created reflects our feelings toward its creator.

THE WORKSHOP OF RESTORATION

I remember the year of my adolescence when I was hit by the creative fever. I call it a fever because it truly seemed like I was sick.

I couldn't stop experimenting with wires, plaster, wood, and nails. My room smelled like glue, and I had paint on my nails. I wanted to create.

Looking back, most of my creations were of questionable beauty. I remember my mother, however, taking my creations and placing them in a showcase alongside her porcelain vases and glass figurines, her place for displaying beautiful and valuable objects.

Why did my mother do that? Because she knew that the way she treated my creations would reflect what she felt about me. In fact, she still keeps some of them, although I tell her she should burn them.

In the first chapter of Genesis, the Bible says that God created human beings in His image. The author makes it very clear that, despite all of creation reflecting the glory of its creator, there's something that distinguishes humans from minerals, plants, and animals. In a different and intentional way, God imprinted His image on human beings, not only shaping them from the dust of the earth like an artist molds their work from clay but also kissing the dust, breathing His essence into it. Humans, from the very beginning, bear the divine image.

But how could Gomer reflect the image of God? How is it possible that there was a divine image, something worthy of value, in a promiscuous, sick, and enslaved woman? In the same way that there is value imprinted on a hundred-euro bill that has fallen into a pit of excrement. Even if that bill is wrinkled, dirty, and foul-smelling, as long as that bill exists, it holds value. There is an image printed on it that makes it valuable. Similarly, even if a person has been abused, violated, or is ill, even if their mind is filled with lies, they engage in destructive habits, or have a corrupted character, as long as that person exists, they have value. Their condition doesn't determine their worth. Those who understand this are capable of reaching into the most repugnant places to rescue what is valuable.

We must then decide whether we will become restorers or destroyers of the image of God in others, because that's what relationships are about. When a human being is mistreated, objectified, or ignored, those actions become actions against God. It's a disregard for the image they bear, an offense to their creator.

On the other hand, when we protect someone's dignity, treat them with kindness, or celebrate their virtues, those actions become actions in favor of God. They are a way of showing love to the creator by loving the creation.

Ultimately, when we love Gomer, we love God. When we pay the price for someone to bring them back to us, when we forgive them, fight for connection, strive to stay united, or do anything else that liberates our partner from the slavery of their mistakes, that love becomes redemptive. In this way, we collaborate with God in the work of restoration that He initiated on the cross.

Have you ever carefully read the scene in which Pontius Pilate asks the Jews if they prefer Jesus or Barabbas? It's in Matthew 27. I used to hate Barabbas more than anyone else in the Gospel, and I didn't understand why his name had to be there. I thought he was entirely dispensable.

The Bible says that Governor Pilate felt uncomfortable with the idea of sentencing Jesus to death because he found no reason to crucify him. So Pilate thought, "Today is a sacred day for the people, and it's a tradition to release a condemned prisoner. I'll let them choose whom to free and whom to kill."

And here's when I start to feel my gut twist.

Pilate sets up a scandalous auction. He asks the crowd, "Whom do you want me to release, Jesus or Barabbas?" How can such a question even be possible? There's no comparison. It's another shameful auction.

On one side of the stage we have Barabbas. The Bible doesn't tell us a lot about him, but what we know is enough. He's a rebel. He's a wicked man who led a revolt. He's a traitor who deceived many. He's a violent man who killed others. Barabbas deserves the cross, deserves the nails that will pierce his wrists; he deserves death. And Pilate knows it, the people know it, you and I know it.

On the other side of the stage, we have Jesus. What's Jesus' crime? He always spoke the truth. He always showed love. He was always upright. He spent his entire life helping the poor, dignifying prostitutes, healing the sick... So tell me! Why is he wearing those chains, then?

It's a scandalous comparison. A face-off between Jesus and Barabbas: absolute goodness against absolute evil. So Pilate asks the crowd, "Whom do you want me to release?" Astonishingly, the people respond with shouts: "Barabbas! Release Barabbas!"

Or, maybe it's not so surprising.

I can imagine the guards approaching Barabbas' cell, telling him as they open his door, "Today's your lucky day, someone else will carry the cross we had prepared for you." Meanwhile, the crowd keeps chanting Barabbas' name, and he thinks, "Wow! People love me, I'm a national hero."

But how clueless that man is. Barabbas has no idea what's happening. What's occurring is not about him; it's about Jesus. And this is the moment in the story that I hate the most: Barabbas walking out of the cell, celebrating his freedom, crosses paths with Jesus, who begins to carry the cross with his name on it, and guess what?

There's no look of gratitude toward Jesus, no words of consideration; there's not a hint of respect for the one who is taking Barabbas' place. I wish I could enter the scene and just knock him out!

I AM BARABBAS

I always felt anger when reading this episode from the Gospel, until the Spirit of God confronted me in the midst of my fury, saying,

"Enough! You cannot hate whom I have loved."

Those words shook me, deeply stirred my soul.

I could hear Jesus saying to me,

"I loved Barabbas, and I remained silent on that stage so he could go free."

"But Jesus! Barabbas was a wicked man!"

I tried to reason with the voice of God.

"Yes... but I loved him and stayed silent out of love, just as I stayed silent for you," concluded the voice of God.

Then, I could understand what I hadn't grasped before:

I am Barabbas.

He is me, and he is you too.

We can deceive ourselves, saying, "I'm not as bad as Barabbas."
I can console myself by comparing myself to others and feeling

better than them. But the truth is, we don't realize how filthy we are until we compare ourselves to the purity of Jesus.

He always told the truth, while I've polished my lies.

He forgave his offenders, while I justified my resentment.

He gave to the poor, while I coveted my neighbor's wealth.

He loved with purity, while I indulged in lust.

I am more Barabbas than any other character in the Bible.

My perspective has changed. I no longer see the story from the outside; I see it from within. I see myself in that scene, face to face with Jesus, knowing who he is and who I am, absolute goodness against absolute evil.

I know justice is looking for me, but Jesus interrupts, saying,

"Take me. Take me, and set him free."

"No, Jesus! I deserve this! I'm the one at fault! This is my shame!" I shout at the executioners. As they remove my chains and place the cross on his shoulders, Jesus looks at me and says,

"No, Barabbas, let me take this. Let me take your place, let me bear your sin, let me suffer your punishment." And as he carries the cross I deserve, and I receive a pardon I don't comprehend, I see him walking toward the place of his breaking, while I stand there as a free man.

When all of God's justice is about to crush Jesus, his love whispers to me,

"Live, Barabbas, live; I will die for you."

TRUE LOVE

Read these words as you've never read before:

God demonstrated His love for us by sending His only Son into this wicked world to give us eternal life through His death. That is true love. It's not about us loving God, but that He loved us so much that He was willing to send His only Son as an atoning sacrifice for our sins.

1 John 4:9-10 (author's emphasis)

If true love hasn't transformed you yet, it's because you haven't discovered Jesus.

Look at the cross.

Look at Jesus nailed, naked, and torn on that cross, and ask yourself why.

The Gospel says that what kept Jesus nailed to that cross until the end wasn't the nails; it was His love for you.

The scandal of the cross is that it was a substitution. Jesus took your sin and gave you His righteousness, and in doing so, God treated Jesus with the punishment you deserved, so that He could treat you with the honor Jesus deserved.

Jesus died your death so you can live His life. You stand before God's throne as if you were Jesus, because on that cross, Jesus stood before God as if He were you.

> **IF TRUE LOVE HASN'T TRANSFORMED YOU YET, IT'S BECAUSE YOU HAVEN'T DISCOVERED JESUS.**

That is the greatest declaration of love that exists.

That is true love.

And it was for you, Barabbas.

You are loved with a love so real, so intense, unconditional, pure, and eternal, that your mind cannot grasp all its implications.

It's a love that still shocks the universe, that makes angels applaud, demons tremble, theologians marvel philosophers question, poets inspire, and children laugh.

How about living it now?

BIBLIOGRAPHY

- Christophe Galfard. *El Universo en tu mano.* Blackie Books. 2017

- Francis Chan. *Tu y yo por siempre.* Unilit. 2015

- Jaime Fasold. *Tu media naranja.* Editorial Portavoz. 1998

- James Strong. *Concordancia Strong.* Grupo Nelson. 2002

- Josh McDowell. *La verdad desnuda.* Editorial Patmos. 2011

- Rob Bell. *Velvet Elvis.* Zondervan. 2005

- Rob Bell. *Sexo Dios.* Editorial Vida. 2007

- Tim Keller. *Encuentros con Jesús.* Editorial Poiema. 2016

- Tim y Khaty Keller. *El Significado del matrimonio.* Publicaciones Andamio. 2014

SOME QUESTIONS YOU MAY ASK:

WHO IS BEHIND THIS BOOK?
Especialidades 625 is a team of pastors and servants from different countries, different denominations, different church sizes and styles, that love Christ and the new generations.

e625.com

WHAT IS E625.COM ABOUT?
Our passion is to help families and churches in Latin America to find good materials and resources for discipleship of the new generations and that is why our website serves parents, pastors, teachers, and leaders in general 365 days a year through www.e625.com with free resources.

ZONA DE CONTENIDO
PREMIUM

WHAT IS PREMIUM SERVICE?
In addition to reflections and free short materials, we have a service of lessons, series, research, online books, and audiovisual resources to facilitate your task. Your church can access this service per congregation with a monthly subscription that allows all the leaders of a local church to download materials to share as a team and make the necessary copies that they find relevant for the different activities of the congregation or their families.

INSTITUTO

CAN I EQUIP MYSELF WITH YOUR HELP?
It would be a privilege to help you and with that objective we have our events and our possibilities of formal education. Visit www.e625.com/Eventos to find out about our seminars and go www.institutoE625.com to learn about the online courses offered by Instituto e6.25

DO YOU WANT CONTINUOUS UPDATES?
Register right now for e625.com updates depending on your field of work: children, preteens, teens, young adults.

LET'S LEARN TOGETHER!

e625.com

/e625com

Downloads Subscription
Recursos gratis
Store
Chat
Magazine
INSTITUTO
e625
Online Education
www.institutoe625.com
Events
Seminars
Books
e625.com